KT-463-081

PROCEDURE AND THE EUROPEAN COURT

Janet Dine, LLB, PhD, AKC, Barrister

Director of the Centre of European Law,
School of Law, King's College, London University

and

Sionaidh Douglas-Scott, BA (Hons), LLM, Barrister
Ingrid Persaud, LLB, LLM

Centre of European Law
Chancery Law Publishing
London
1991

Published in the United Kingdom by
Chancery Law Publishing Ltd
22 Eastcastle Street
London W1N 7PA

Centre of European Law
King's College London
Strand
London WC2R 2LS

Typeset by August Filmsetting
Haydock, St Helens

Printed in Great Britain by
Ipswich Book Co

ISBN 1-85630-010-2

All rights reserved. No part of this publication may be
reproduced in any form or by any means, electronic,
mechanical, photocopying, recording or otherwise, or
stored in any retrieval system without the written per-
mission of the copyright holders and the publishers

©
Centre of European Law
1991

Contents

DISPOSED OF BY LIBRARY HOUSE OF LORDS

Contents

Cases Cited

Chapter I

European Court Of Justice – an overview*

Over the past few years the pace towards greater integration in Europe has quickened. The provisions of the Single European Act 1986 considerably widened the sphere of competence of the Community, and two intergovernmental conferences, one on economic and monetary union and the other on political union, commenced in December 1990. EC law is supreme over national law, and has been since 1 January 1973 as a result of the European Communities Act 1972, and its scope is being constantly extended. These days, no businessman can neglect its impact, and the lawyer who fails to advise his client on the EC aspects of his case risks giving seriously negligent advice. EC law has brought about changes in fields as diverse as competition and discrimination law, company law and environmental law. Lawyers may have to advise not only on the availability of a defence or remedy under EC law, but also on the means of pursuing it – whether in the national courts or the European Court of Justice, in Luxembourg. The aim of this book is to illustrate the fundamental part played by the European Court in the development of EC law and in particular to highlight major recent developments in the procedure and jurisdiction of the European Court (Chaps 2, 3 and 4).

The European Court

In the making and promulgation of EC law, the European Court plays a crucial role. Many of the fundamental doctrines of EC law are not to be found in the Treaty, or secondary EC legislation, but in the case law of the European Court. For example, in 1962, in the case of *Van Gend en Loos*, the Court introduced the doctrine of direct effect, one of the keystones of EC law, which gives the individual the right to pursue an EC remedy in the national courts. It was in this case that the European Court referred to EC law as a "new legal order". The introduction of the doctrine of direct effect also provides an excellent example of the policy approach of the Court. By encouraging individuals to bring actions in national courts on the basis of what the European Court has decided are directly effective provisions, the European Court can supervise the development of EC law at national level, despite the fact that Article 177 gives the European Court only the role of interpreting EC law.

Furthermore, since the EEC Treaty (unlike the European Coal and Steel Community (ECSC) Treaty) is drafted to provide the broad framework of Community law rather than its details, the European Court has been very influential in filling in any gaps, in a way that may be surprising to English lawyers. The Court has often given effect to what it perceives to be the spirit rather than the letter of EC law – in some cases coming to a decision almost in defiance of the wording of the Treaty (see for example, Case 294/83 *Parti Ecologiste "Les Verts" v European Parliament* [1987] 2 CMLR 343, mentioned below).

The European Court has not been slow to develop specific remedies and procedures available under EC law, as the papers in this collection show. The European Court has to ensure that "in the interpretation and application of this treaty the law is observed" (Art 164 EEC Treaty). In this respect, the Court has a very wide-ranging role; ensuring that the Council and Commission keep within their powers under the Treaty and, additionally, restraining Member States who act in breach of the Treaties. The European Court has also been responsible for breaking new ground in areas of substantive law, for example in the discrimination field (Case 43/75 *Defrenne v Sabena (No 2)* [1976] ECR 455) or in the area of free movement of goods (Case 120/78 *"Cassis de Dijon"* [1979] ECR 649).

Some writers have even felt that the Court may have been responsible for breaking too much new ground in all areas, and this has led to charges that the European Court has been guilty of "judicial activism". However, "activism", if it was such, may have been no bad thing, when development of Community law by other institutions was proceeding very slowly (in the 1970s, for example).

Thus, the Court is provided by the Treaties with an extremely wide jurisdiction. It serves, in a sense, as an international court, hearing suits brought against Member States for alleged Treaty violations (Art 169

EEC Treaty). It also acts as an administrative court, exercising a power of judicial review over Community legislation (Arts 173–176, Art 184 EEC Treaty) and can annul Community acts. It can also entertain actions brought against Community institutions for damages (Arts 178, 215 EEC Treaty). It has the extremely important power to give preliminary rulings on questions of interpretation or validity of Community law when so requested by the courts of Member States (Art 177 EEC Treaty). Most of these heads of jurisdiction are examined and recent developments explored.

Indeed, the Court has recently become so overburdened by its heavy case load that in 1989 a new Court of First Instance was set up (by Art 11 of the Single European Act and the new Art 168A of the EEC Treaty) to deal with some of its work, primarily competition and staff cases. *Tim Millett*'s chapter deals with the Court of First Instance in detail, explaining how it operates, and the basis of its jurisdiction. However, the workload of the European Court continues to rise, partly as the heightened awareness of the 1992 programme leads to a resurgence of EC litigation, partly as the new Member States, Spain and Portugal, take advantage of EC remedies, particularly the Article 177 procedure. The European Court continues, in this way, to be a victim of its own success.

Composition and organization of the European Court

The Court is made up of 13 judges (one from each Member State and a President) assisted by six Advocates-General. They are chosen by the unanimous agreement of the governments of the Member States. The 10 official languages of the Member States are those of the Court, which has substantial interpreting and translation facilities, although French is the working language of the court.

The Court is divided into six "Chambers", thus enabling smaller groups of judges to deal with cases of lesser importance, and helping the Court to cope with its increasing workload. A Registrar deals with the procedure and administration of the Court. The Registrar plays a much more important role than in the English court system and sits with the other judges on the Bench, but takes no part in the judgment. Each Judge and Advocate-General has a "Cabinet", or team of legal experts and secretaries working exclusively for him.

The Advocate-General's role is to assist the Court by presenting "submissions" *i.e.* a reasoned opinion and recommendations on the case before it. The Court does not always follow his opinion, although it may be invoked as a persuasive authority in subsequent cases. His opinion may also shed some light on the judgment of the Court itself. This is because the judges act as a collegiate body and reach a single judgment – there are no separate or dissenting opinions. The attempt to achieve uniformity may sometimes result in a judgment being somewhat equivocal and the Advocate-General's opinion may provide a more expansive account of the case.

Precedent and interpretation in the Court

The doctrine of precedent does not operate in the strict sense in the European Court. Although the Court follows its previous decisions in the majority of cases, it is free to depart from them where it feels necessary. In such cases the Court will simply ignore previous case law.

One of the principal tasks of the Court is the interpretation of the Treaties and secondary Community legislation. However, the Court uses different techniques of interpretation to those used in English courts. Although it looks at the words of the provision to be interpreted, and considers their meaning in the context of the instrument as a whole, its approach is far more purposive than that of the common law courts. It often interprets texts on the basis of the overall general aims of the Community. This approach has been attacked by some as usurping the legislative function. However, given that EC legislation is drafted quite differently to English statutes, with a greater degree of abstraction, there is less scope for the literal approach to statutory interpretation employed by English judges.

Practice and procedure

Notwithstanding the success and influence of the European Court, many lawyers in this country are unaware of its practice and procedure. A sound grasp of European Court practice is becoming increasingly important as, not only do lawyers here now face the prospect of advising a client whether he has *locus standi* to bring his case in the

European Court, but also the possibility of having to represent his client in that court too, for both solicitors and barristers have rights of audience there.

Given the history and development of the European Community, the practice and procedure of the European Court of Justice is very different to that of our common law courts. Unlike the system in operation in the United Kingdom, which is oral and adversarial in character, proceedings in the European Court are largely written, and, if anything, inquisitorial in nature. This is partly because procedure in the European Court is very loosely modelled on continental models, such as that of the French Conseil d'Etat and the International Court of Justice in the Hague. The United Kingdom was not a member of the Community in the 1950's and 60's and thus unable to influence the development of the Court's procedure in its early days. However, there are good practical reasons why the European Court should rely heavily on written proceedings. As a major institution of a Community which spans 12 countries and 10 languages, with no single language in common, the Court has to rely heavily on interpreters, as not all judges will be familiar with the language of the case. There is thus very little scope for any great displays of advocacy, especially as counsel are required to restrict the length of their address to 30 minutes. The judges read the papers in advance of the hearing and consequently counsel's role is limited. However, by reducing oral hearings to the minimum, time and money are saved. This is of great importance at a time when the European Court has a very heavy case load. Interestingly, the greater use of written proceedings has been considered as a means of reducing cost and delay in national court proceedings (for example by the Lord Chancellor's Civil Justice Review, which made its final report in 1988).

The European Court has the power to order interim measures in the course of proceedings before it (Art 186 EEC Treaty and Arts 83, 84 of the Rules of Procedure of the Court). For example, interim relief may be granted to a company that is appealing against a Commission decision in a competition case. In Case 27/76R *United Brands* [1976] ECR 245, two provisions of a Commission decision were suspended by the Court until it could give judgment on the appeal from that decision. However, the Court will not order interim measures "unless there are circumstances giving rise to urgency and factual and legal grounds establishing a prima facie case for the measures applied for" (Art 83,

Rules of Procedure). These conditions are very hard to satisfy, as is evidenced by the fact that very few applications for interim measures are made each year, and only a small percentage of these are successful.

One major flaw in European Court procedure seems to be the fact that the Court has no effective way of enforcing its judgments. In particular, judgments against Member States for failure to fulfil their obligations under the EEC Treaty are only declaratory in status (although under the ECSC Treaty the Court has the power to impose sanctions on recalcitrant Member States). This can sometimes be a problem – in 1988, 93 previous decisions of the Court had not been fully complied with. It seems somewhat paradoxical that a court which has the power to give such far-reaching rulings is unable to enforce its judgments in some cases.

Jurisdiction

As already mentioned this is wide-ranging and provides the Court with many functions, although it should be remembered that the Court's jurisdiction, and thus the remedies it may provide, is entirely circumscribed by the Treaties. However, in recent years, the European Court has on occasion appeared unworried by the wording of the Treaties, sometimes finding a base of jurisdiction where none appears in the Treaties, as *John Usher*'s chapter shows.

The jurisdiction of the European Court falls roughly under the following headings.

A. *Preliminary rulings*

These concern actions brought by individuals in the national courts. Problems of interpretation of Community law which arise in the course of litigation in the national courts may be referred to the European Court.

B. *Actions against Member States*

These may be brought either by the Commission, or by another Member State, where a Member State fails to fulfil an obligation under the Treaties.

C. Actions against Community institutions

These comprise judicial review of Community action (or inaction) actions for damages and actions brought by Community staff.

The cases brought under the last two headings are direct actions which start and end in the European Court. The preliminary ruling procedure is, however, only an indirect way of proceeding in the European Court, as the action starts in the national court, and returns there for determination after the European Court has given its ruling.

Outside these headings, issues of Community law may be raised in the national courts, in the course of any litigation in which they are relevant. This is very important, given that the right of an individual to pursue an action in the European Court is very limited, as will be seen. If the Community is to provide an effective system of remedies, it is essential that national courts play their part in the promulgation of EC law, and the development of the doctrine of direct effect by the European Court has made this possible.

Preliminary rulings

These lie at the core of the system of judicial remedies provided under EEC law, and *Richard Whish*'s chapter explores the relevant law and procedure in detail.

Article 177 provides that if, before any national court or tribunal, a question arises as to the:

(a) interpretation of the EEC Treaty; or
(b) validity or interpretation of acts of the institutions of the Community; or
(c) interpretations of the statutes of bodies established by the Council, where such statutes so provide

and a decision on that question is necessary to enable it to give judgment, then that court or tribunal may, and indeed must if it is a court or tribunal against whose decisions no judicial remedy is available, make a reference to the European Court.

Article 177 provides the main link between the courts of the Member States and the European Court. If Community law is to be truly effective, it is essential that it can be pleaded and relied upon in the courts of

Member States, which are more accessible to individuals, as well as in the European Court. The doctrine of direct effect ensures that it can. In fact, because the European Court's jurisdiction is circumscribed by the Treaties, any disputes involving Community law which fall outside the European Court's jurisdiction must be decided in the national courts. And thus disputes between individuals, or companies, or between private parties and the national authorities, rather than Community institutions, will never directly come before the European Court. However, the preliminary ruling procedure provides a mechanism for national courts to refer problems of the interpretation and validity of EC law to the European Court, where a decision on that question is necessary to enable the national court to give judgment. All proceedings in the national court are stayed pending the ruling but continue afterwards on the basis of the European Court's decision. This procedure ensures uniformity in the application of Community law in all national legal systems. It lies at the foundation of the constitutional order of the EC, and the European Court's role in this context has been described as that of a transnational constitutional court. Many of the most important cases decided by the European Court were decided in the context of a preliminary ruling, *e.g.* Case 26/62 *Van Gend en Loos* [1963] ECR 1, Case 6/64 *Costa* v *ENEL* [1964] ECR 585, Case 43/75 *Defrenne* v *Sabena* [1976] ECR 455.

The need for such a procedure is particularly obvious in the case of rulings on validity, where the supremacy of Community law would be threatened if national courts could pronounce it invalid. There would also be the possibility of great confusion caused by one national court declaring a piece of Community legislation valid, and another invalid. Although under Article 177 the European Court is not given exclusive jurisdiction to declare Community legislation invalid, in Case 314/85 *Firma Foto-Frost* [1988] 3 CMLR 57, the European Court held that the national courts had no such power, stating:

> "Divergences between courts in the Member States as to the validity of Community acts would be liable to place in jeopardy the very unity of the Community legal order and detract from the fundamental requirement of legal certainty."

Preliminary rulings account for nearly half of the workload of the Court. While the Treaty required that Article 177 references be heard in full court, in plenary session and not by a Chamber (Art 165(2) EEC Treaty) thus stressing their importance, in practice, pressure of work under Article 177 has forced the Court to hear these cases in Chambers, thus abandoning this requirement. Some concern has been expressed at the fact that preliminary rulings are still taking up to two years to be determined by the Court, notwithstanding the setting up of the Court of First Instance, which siphons off other work. This delay is especially worrying in the context of preliminary rulings, which are just a stage in the national court procedure, and do not finally determine the case. Any delay which is therefore likely to discourage litigants from considering its use is not to be welcomed.

However, there are means by which unnecessary references can be weeded out. Before a national judge can refer a question of Community law to the European Court he must feel that the determination of that question is necessary to enable him to give judgment. In Case 283/81 *CILFIT* [1982] ECR 3415, the European Court set out the conditions under which it would be unnecessary for a court of last resort to refer a question of European law to the European Court (however, these conditions apply equally to lower courts who are trying to determine whether a reference is necessary). These were:

  (i) where the question of EEC law is irrelevant;

 (ii) where the question raised was materially identical to one on which the European Court had already given a ruling;

(iii) where the correct application of Community law was so obvious as to leave no reasonable doubt as to the way in which the question raised should be resolved.

In setting this condition the European Court came close to sanctioning the doctrine of *acte clair* (which means roughly that where the meaning of a provision is clear there is no need for interpretation). However, the Court also added that before a national court came to this conclusion it should bear in mind the objectives and special nature of Community law, and also that Community legislation is drafted in several different languages which make comparisons difficult. By adding these qualifications the Court seemed to be almost killing off the possibility of the *acte clair* doctrine applying.

In general, the case law on Article 177 arises in the following areas. Firstly, there may be some doubt as to whether the court or tribunal which seeks to make the reference actually qualifies as a "court or tribunal" for the purposes of Article 177 – in these cases the European Court tries to determine whether that body exercises a judicial function. Secondly, courts or tribunals which are not those of final resort have an unfettered discretion in the matter of referral. What criteria then should the national court adopt in deciding whether to make a reference? Basically, it seems that the national court should consider that a decision on a question of Community law is *necessary* to enable it to give judgment (the *CILFIT* guidelines will be of help here). If a decision is necessary, then the judge must decide whether, in his discretion he should refer. Factors such as the heavy work load of the Court of Justice might justify a decision not to refer in a straightforward case. Finally, where the court or tribunal concerned is one against whose decisions there is no judicial remedy under national law, Article 177(3) requires that "that court or tribunal shall bring the matter before the Court of Justice", *i.e.* that court, unlike lower courts, has no discretion. In England a particular problem arises in this situation as there is no automatic right of appeal from the Court of Appeal to the House of Lords. So in England, the court of last instance in many cases would be the Court of Appeal. *Richard Whish*'s chapter explores all of these issues in depth.

It should be remembered that there is inherent in Article 177 a division of competence – the European Court has the power to interpret Community law but not to apply it to the facts of the case. That is for the national courts. In Case 6/64 *Costa* v *ENEL* [1964] ECR 585, the Court emphasised that Article 177.

> "gives the Court no jurisdiction either to apply the Treaty to a specific case or to decide upon the validity of a provision of domestic law in relation to the Treaty, as it would be possible for it to do under Article 169."

The dividing line between interpretation and application is, however, very fine. In some cases the European Court has given such a precise and detailed judgment that virtually no leeway has been left to the national courts in implementing it. In Case 129/79 *Macarthys Ltd* v *Smith* [1980] ECR 1275, the European Court held that Article 119 proscribed sex discrimination over pay in situations of sequential employment as well as contemporaneous employment, and this effectively decided the case. However, more recently, the European Court has tended to stress the national court's role in applying Community law.

Given that some of the most important doctrines of Community law have been established by preliminary rulings of the European Court, there is a serious question as to what the effect of these rulings should be. Should they take effect retroactively, *i.e.* as also applying to legal relationships arising before the date of judgment, or should they apply only to the present case in hand and to future cases? In Case 43/75 *Defrenne* v *Sabena (No 2)* [1976] ECR 455, the European Court agreed to limit the effect of its ruling on Article 119 to the present case and future cases, bearing in mind the arguments of the British and Irish governments that a retrospective application of the equal pay principle would have serious economic consequences. In this way the effect of its judgment resembled the doctrine of prospective overruling applied by the US Supreme Court. However, this case seems to be exceptional and in Case 811/79 *Ariete SpA* [1980] ECR 2545, the Court made it clear that a ruling under Article 177 should normally be applied to legal relationships arising prior to the date of judgment.

Thus, the Article 177 procedure enables individuals to circumvent their limited rights of *locus standi* before the Court of Justice by bringing proceedings in their own national courts instead. It also provides for uniformity in the interpretation of Community law, and for co-operation between national courts and the European Court, although "co-operation" may mean very little to the individual litigant, who has no say in whether the reference is made and has to rely on the discretion of the court. Finally, the preliminary ruling procedure has provided the European Court with an opportunity to give some of its most important and far-reaching judgments.

Actions against Member States

Although these are not specifically covered it seems wise to mention them in this introduction and thus to give a complete picture of the Court's jurisdiction. The Community cannot function properly if Member States disregard their obligations under it, by, for example, failing to implement a Directive within the time limit, or by violating basic Treaty provisions, *i.e.* by imposing an import ban contrary to the Treaty provisions on free movement of goods. In cases such as these, the European Court operates as an International Court, by hearing suits brought against the Member State in question. There are two ways in which action may be taken against a Member State which fails to fulfil an obligation under the Treaty. Proceedings may be taken either by the Commission (Art 169 EEC Treaty) or by another Member State (Art 170 EEC Treaty) and the procedure is similar in both cases.

Under Article 169, the Commission acts as Community watchdog, although its powers are discretionary; it need not take any action if it feels it is unnecessary. At first, the Commission will write to the Member State concerned, warning it of its breach and asking for comments. If this does not settle the matter (and it often does) the formal procedure under Article 169 has three stages. First, the Commission formally asks the State for its observations on that view, after which the Commission will deliver a reasoned opinion. If the State fails to take remedial action within the specified time, the Commission will bring the case before the European Court. The Court will then give judgment if it feels that there has been a failure to fulfil a Treaty obligation. However, (as mentioned earlier) under Article 171 (EEC Treaty) this judgment is only declaratory. Although the State is required "to take the necessary measures to comply with the judgment" under Article 171, there are no sanctions for non-compliance. If the State concerned fails to comply, the Commission may bring a second action, claiming that failure to comply with the Court's judgment is itself a Treaty violation. This happened in Case 232/78 *Commission* v *France* [1979] ECR 2729 (the "Sheepmeat" case) in which France refused to import lamb and mutton from the United Kingdom, thus infringing Community rules on free movement of goods. When France refused to comply with the first judgment, the Commission brought a second action against it, applying to the Court for interim measures at the same time. However, the Court refused to entertain this application for interim measures, claiming that they would not be necessary as required by Article 186 of the EEC Treaty, as any judgment it gave would substantially duplicate its previous one. It may well be that the Court realised that there was little chance of France complying with another judgment and simply wanted to save face by not having its authority ignored for a second time. The Court's inability to impose sanctions (except in the context of the ECSC Treaty) does, however, present something of a problem, although States do usually (eventually) comply. Indeed, in most cases, States seek to avoid a judgment against them, which after all does represent "a documented record of intrusion upon their sovereignty" (Everling).

Since the passing of the Single European Act, the Commission has announced that its top priority under Article 169 will be to concentrate on unilateral measures taken by Member States, in breach of Article 100A(4), in areas which should instead be subject to Community harmonisation.

One Member State may also bring an action against another under Article 170. However, the matter must first be brought before the Commission, which may in fact take over the proceedings under Article 169. That the Commission should do this is desirable, for in a Community that is supposedly made up of Member States with common interests, and good relations, direct confrontation between Member States in court is obviously best avoided. In fact, only one such case has proceeded to judgment – this concerned a dispute between France and the United Kingdom over fishing legislation.

Actions against Community institutions

This is an important and confusing head of jurisdiction of the European Court and merits detailed consideration. Community legislation is binding not only on Member States. It also considerably affects individuals, and the way they order their lives. Community law creates rights and obligations which may be of great benefit to individuals. However, Community institutions also daily take decisions which affect the very livelihood of individuals and companies within the EC, such as whether to fine a company for violation of EC competition law (the fine can be up to 10% of annual turnover) whether to grant a licence to import goods into the EC, or whether to impose a subsidy on certain products. Furthermore, since the Single European Act, the competence of Community institutions has considerably increased. However, the Community's law-making powers are quite narrowly circumscribed. The kinds of decision that may be taken by Community institutions, and methods of implementation are carefully prescribed. Each Community institution must act within the limits of powers conferred upon it by the Treaties, or by secondary Community legislation. It is of great importance that all Community institutions respect the requirements set out in the Treaties, for, if this were not the case, the Member States might not have been willing to transfer such wide powers to the Community at all.

The Treaties also give the Court of Justice the jurisdiction to control the way the other institutions exercise their power. Unlike in the UK legal system, where courts do not have the power to review Acts of Parliament, the European Court of Justice may even, under certain circumstances, annul the acts of other Community institutions. Furthermore, decisions of the European Court cannot themselves be annulled by the Commission or Council, in contrast to judgments of the House of Lords, which may be reversed by Act of Parliament. So, in ensuring that the Community institutions act according to the rule of law (as they are obliged to do by Art 4 of the EEC Treaty) the European Court plays an important role.

It is the task of the Court to ensure that in the interpretation and application of the Treaties the law is observed (Art 164 EEC Treaty). This entails the review of the legality of Community act – *i.e.* whether the institution had the power to issue the act concerned, whether it followed the correct procedures and for the right reasons. The Court has this power under Article 173 of the EEC Treaty. If legislation passed by a Community institution is invalid, the Court has the power to annul the act concerned. The Court also has the power to review the other institutions' inactivity or failure to act (under Art 175 EEC Treaty) to hear actions for damages brought by those who have suffered loss as a result of Community legislation (Arts 178, 215 EEC Treaty). In the course of hearing such actions the Court frequently examines the legality of Community legislation. Through this power of review the Court is able to scrutinise fairly closely the actions of the other institutions. Each of these procedures will be considered.

Article 173

Article 173 of the EEC Treaty (and Article 33 of the ECSC Treaty) permits the Court to annul acts of the Council or Commission which violate Community law.

Article 173 provides:

> "The Court of Justice shall review the legality of acts of the Council and the Commission other than recommendations or opinions. It shall for this purpose have jurisdiction in an action brought by a Member State, the Council

or the Commission on grounds of lack of competence, infringement of an essential procedural requirement, infringement of this Treaty or of any rule of law relating to its application, or misuse of powers.

Any natural or legal person may, under the same conditions, institute proceedings against a decision addressed to that person or against a decision, which, although in the form of a Regulation or Decision addressed to another person, is of direct and individual concern to the former.

The proceedings provided for in this Article shall be instituted within two months of the publication of the measure, or of its notification to the plaintiff, or, in the absence thereof, of the day on which it came to the knowledge of the latter, as the case may be."

In order to succeed in an application for judicial review under Article 173 the applicant must satisfy these four grounds:
(a) there must be a reviewable act – *i.e.* one that is capable of having legal effects;
(b) the applicant must have *locus standi*;
(c) the action must be brought within the time limits set out in Article 173;
(d) the applicant must be entitled to succeed on the merits.

Reviewable acts

Not all types of act passed by Community institutions are susceptible to judicial review – recommendations and opinions are expressly excluded by Article 173. However, reviewable acts are not confined to Regulations, Directives or Decisions (which, unlike Recommendations or Opinions, have binding force, according to Article 189, which details the types of act that Community institutions may pass "to carry out their task"). Instead, all measures which are binding, or designed to have legal effects, may be reviewed by the Court.

In Cases 8–11/66 *Re Noordwijk's Cement Accoord* [1967] ECR 75, the act challenged was a letter sent to the applicant by the Commission under Regulation 17, which stated that the applicant's immunity from fines was at an end as it was thought to be breaching Community competition law. The Commission argued that the letter contained no more than an opinion and was not a decision. The Court disagreed, stating (at p 91):

"... the said measure affected the interests of the undertakings by bringing about a distinct change in their legal position. It is unequivocally a measure which produces legal effects touching the interests of the undertakings concerned and which is binding them. It thus constitutes not a mere opinion but a decision."

Therefore, the Court looks at the substance and nature of the act, rather than at what it is called. In Case 60/81 *IBM* [1981] ECR 2639, the Court held that a statement of objections by the Commission, stating that IBM was in breach of a dominant position under Article 86 of the EEC competition rules, did not amount to a reviewable act. It was simply a preliminary decision which could be challenged only in the course of review of the final decision. However, the European Court confirmed that it is the substance of the act, and not its label, which is important, stating: ". . . the form in which such acts or decisions are cast is, in principle, immaterial as regards the question whether they are open to challenge".

Article 173 refers only to acts of the Council and Commission. However, the Court has held the acts of the European Parliament are also subject to review. In Case 294/83 *Partie Ecologiste "Les Verts"* v *European Parliament* [1987] 2 CMLR 343, the Court held that the European Parliament's decision, allocating funds for the European Parliament electorial campaign of 1984, could be reviewed in the context of Article 173. The European Court justified this decision on the basis that since the drafting of the EEC Treaty, the European Parliament's powers had grown. While originally the Parliament had only the right to be consulted on legislation, and a certain amount of political control over other Community institutions, it now had he right to take actions which were binding on third parties. Thus, notwithstanding the wording of Article 173, its actions *ought* to be reviewable. This judgment has been criticised on the basis that the European Court was substituting its own (policy based) view for that of the Treaties and has been cited as an example of the Court's judicial "activism".

Locus standi

As well as restrictions on the types of acts that may be reviewed, there are restrictions on those who have the right to bring the action. In particular, there are stringent requirements of *locus standi* concerning individual applicants. This is understandable, otherwise the Court might be swamped by individual applicants who wished to challenge Community measures which they claimed had affected them.

Under Article 173, the Member States, the Council and the Commission are designated privileged applicants. If they wish to contest the legality of a Community act they need not show any special interest or concern in it, as they are already deemed to have sufficient interest by virtue of their status within the Community. The European Parliament is not specifically mentioned in Article 173, so one might have thought that it could not have claimed the status of privileged applicant. However, in its judgment in Case C-70/88 *Parliament* v *Council* (judgment of 22 May 1990) the Court broke new ground. While confirming that under Article 173 of the EEC Treaty and Article 146 of the Euratom Treaty (which are virtually identical) the Parliament is not normally entitled to bring an action for annulment when other legal remedies are available to the Member States, individuals and the Commission (whose responsibility it is to see that the Parliament's prerogatives are respected) the European Court found that in this case the system of remedies provided under the Treaty had not proved effective.

Therefore, an action for annulment brought by the European Parliament against an act of the Commission or Council would be admissable provided that the Parliament sought only to protect its prerogatives by so doing. This ruling was in direct contrast to the Court's earlier ruling in Case 302/87 *European Parliament* v *Council* [1988] ECR 5615. Case 70/88 has been criticised by some as a policy-based re-writing of the Treaty on the part of the European Court (like that of Case 294/83 *Partie Ecologiste "Les Verts"*). (For further comment see p 35.) However, as the Parliament's powers continue to grow (for example, they were substantially increased by the Single European Act) it seems inevitable that its standing before the Court should not in some way be increased.

Natural and legal persons (non-privileged applicants) have very limited standing before the European Court. Article 173 paragraph 2 states that:

> "Any natural or legal person may ... institute proceedings against a decision addressed to that person or against a decision which although in the form of a regulation or a decision addressed to another person, is of direct and individual concern to the former."

In effect this means that non-privileged applicants, should they wish to challenge a Community act in the European Court, must show either:

   (i) the act concerned is a Decision addressed to the applicant; or
  (ii) the act concerned is a Decision addressed to someone else; or
 (iii) the act concerned is in fact a Decision (although in the form of a Regulation).

In cases (ii) and (iii) the applicant must also show that the measure in question is of direct and individual concern to him.

Decisions addressed to the applicant
These cause few problems as far as *locus standi* is concerned. Provided that the act affects the legal position of the applicant, it is in substance a decision. Many such cases are brought in the substantive field of competition law, where undertakings seek to challenge Commission decisions addressed to them, especially those which impose large fines.

Decisions addressed to another person/Decisions in the form of a Regulation
In these cases, as well as showing that it is a true *Decision* that he seeks to challenge, the applicant must show that it is of *direct and individual concern* to him.

    This is one of the most complicated areas of Community law.

The act must in substance be a Decision
Many of the Commission's policies are implemented by directly applicable Regulations. Regulations are essentially legislative, laying down general rules which automatically become part of the legal system of Member States (Art 189 EEC Treaty). They are binding in their entirety and have a wide-ranging effect on individuals and companies, particularly now that the 1992 programme involves a stepping up of legislation. However, a non-privileged applicant cannot challenge a true Regulation. This is partly because implementation of Community policy would become unworkable if such acts were likely to be annulled at the suit of individuals. It is also for reasons of legal certainty – many individuals and companies rely on the provisions of Regulations, and order their affairs accordingly.

    However, whether the measure in question is in fact a "true" Regulation involves a subtle enquiry. The European Court will look at the substance of the act, rather than at what it is called. True Regulations are normative acts – *i.e.* they are acts of general application, rather than concerning designated persons individually, as decisions do. In Cases

16, 17/62 *Confédération National des Producteurs de Fruits et Légumes* [1962] ECR 471, the European Court held:

> "The essential characteristics of a decision arise from the limitation of the persons to whom it is addressed, whereas a regulation, being essentially of a legislative nature, is applicable not to limited number of persons defined or identifiable, but to categories of persons viewed abstractly and in their entirety."

In Cases 41–44/70 *International Fruit Company* [1971] ECR 411, the applicants, a group of fruit importers, were able to challenge a Commission Regulation, which laid down the quantity of import licences for apples to be issued for a certain period. The Commission controlled the number of licences to be issued on the basis of the number of applications received the previous week. Although the figures were enacted by Regulation, it applied only to a finite number of people and it was issued in response to their applications. The Court held that the Commission, although it had acted by Regulation, was in fact issuing Decisions to those who had applied for licences. Therefore, what was called a Regulation was in fact a disguised bundle of Decisions addressed to each applicant.

The European Court has also held that a Regulation may be hybrid in nature. In some cases, a measure having legislative character may also be in the nature of a decision for a certain specified individual, thus enabling him the challenge it. For example, in Cases 113, 118–121/77 *Japanese Ball-Bearings* [1979] 2 CMLR 257 the European Court held that four major Japanese producers of ball-bearings could challenge an anti-dumping Regulation since they were actually named in the Regulation itself. Cases 239, 275/82 *Allied Corporation* [1984] ECR 1005 established that an exporter may be able to challenge an anti-dumping regulation if he took part in the preliminary investigation.

Where the measure which is being challenged is described as a decision, the Court will not seek to re-classify it, even if it is of general application.

The applicant must be able to show direct and individual concern
These requirements restrict the right to apply for annulment of a measure to those who have a clear interest in the case. They have been interpreted very restrictively by the European Court.

Direct concern. A measure will only be of direct concern to an applicant if there is a direct link between the Decision and the application of the Decision to the applicant. It must leave the addressee of the Decision (which will usually be a Member State) no real measure of discretion as to how it is implemented. For example, in Case 69/69 *Alcan* [1970] ECR 385, the applicant, a Belgian aluminium producer, was not able to challenge a Commission Decision refusing to increase the allocation of low-tariff aluminium to Belgium, because the Belgian Government would have had a discretion as to how it distributed the quotas among firms.

However, more recently, the Court seems to be taking a less restrictive approach. In Case 11/82 *Piraiki-Patraiki* [1985] ECR 207, Advocate-General Verloren van Themaat said that a Community measure would be of direct concern provided that its legal effects on interested parties and their identity could with certainty, or a high degree of probability be inferred.

Individual concern. This is very difficult to establish and very few applicants manage to satisfy the Court as to this criteria. Because of this, it is usually the first requirement to be examined by the Court.

The test for individual concern was laid down in Case 25/62 *Plaumann* [1963] ECR 95, where the Court stated (at p 107):

> "Persons other than those to whom a decision is addressed may only claim to be individually concerned if that decision affects them by reason of certain attributes which are peculiar to them or by reason of circumstances in which they are differentiated from all other persons and by virtue of these factors distinguishes them individually just as in the case of the person addressed."

What then are the "characteristics peculiarly relevant to him" which the applicant must prove exist?

First, the cases seem to suggest that to be successful, an applicant needs to show that he was a member of a closed or fixed and identifiable group which no-one else could enter at the time the decision was made. That factor may differentiate him from others, as in the case of *Bock* [1971] ECR 897. Bock had applied for a permit to import Chinese mushrooms into West Germany. They were already in free circulation in other Member States, so the German Government needed the Commission's authority to refuse imports, which it duly got. The European Court found Bock individually concerned by the Commission's decision, as one of those affected by its retrospective character whose identity was fixed and ascertainable at the time the decision was made.

Other cases seem to suggest a relaxation of such strict criteria but can perhaps be explained by their special circumstances. For example, in Case 264/82 *Timex* [1985] ECR 849, Timex was able to establish individual concern by showing that although the act complained of (an anti-dumping Regulation) was not addressed to them, that it was nonetheless issued in proceedings in which they played a legitimate part, as a complainant. In Case 294/83 *Parti Ecologiste "Les Verts"* v *European Parliament* [1987] 2 CMLR 343, the Court held that the Green Party was individually concerned in the European Parliament's decision which had allocated funds for the 1984 European Parliament elections, even although they belonged to a class whose members could not be identified at the date the decision was taken. The Court's decision seems to have been expressly dictated by what policy required. (This case also established that the European Parliament's acts could be reviewed under Article 173 — see above.)

However, these cases cannot be interpreted as indicating that the European Court has abandoned its generally rigorous approach to the requirement of individual concern. In other cases, where the applicant has been able to establish a fairly close link between the measure passed and his situation, he had still failed. In Case 231/82 *Spijker Kwasten* [1983] ECR 2559, the Commission passed a measure, at the request of the Dutch Government, authorising it to ban the import of Chinese brushes for a six month period. This import ban seemed to have been prompted by Spijker's application for a licence to import them, since he was the only person to import Chinese brushes into the Netherlands, and was suspected of having committed a major fraud (and thus it was thought desirable to put a stop to his activities). The European Court nonetheless held that he lacked individual concern, as anyone could apply for licences during that same period. Even if the applicant can establish that he is the only person likely to be affected by the measure in question, this will not be sufficient, provided that the category is not closed and others may enter the field.

A denial of *locus standi* may not of course be the end of the case. The applicant may be able to bring an alternative action in the national courts, using the preliminary reference procedure under Article 177 to establish invalidity of the measure in question. This is exactly what happened in Cases 103, 145/77 *RSH* [1978] ECR 2037, where the plaintiff succeeded in getting a declaration of invalidity under Article 177, having failed to establish *locus standi* under Article 173 (also see below, under actions for damages).

But in some cases, an action in the national courts may not be possible. No doubt, the European Court's restrictive application of the *locus standi* provisions of Article 173 results from a fear of opening floodgates. At a time when the European Court is already overburdened with work, this fear is justified. However, the result of this policy is that in some cases the applicant is left without a remedy, other than lobbying a local MP or MEP. As Community legislation becomes ever more pervasive, this may be a cause for concern.

Time limits

According to Article 173 paragraph 3, actions (whether brought by privileged or non-privileged applicants) must be brought within two months of either:
- the publication of the act;
- its notification to the applicant; or
- the day on which it came to his knowledge.

Grounds on which the act may be annulled

Of course, it is not sufficient just for an applicant to show that he is directly and individually concerned by a measure. He must also show that there is something wrong with it – a ground on which it may be annulled. Article 173 paragraph 1 sets out four such substantive grounds for review. If the Court finds that any one or more of these has been satisfied it will annul the measure in question.

1. Lack of competence

This roughly corresponds to the English concept of substantive *ultra vires*. This means that an institution cannot do anything which it has no power to do under the Treaties or secondary Community legislation.

2. Infringement of an essential procedural requirement

Community institutions must also follow the correct procedures, such as those set out in Article 190 of the EEC Treaty which requires that all secondary legislation state the reasons on which it is based, and the opinions which were required to be obtained. As Case 24/62 *Germany* v *Commission* [1963] ECR 63 shows, the requirements of Article 190 will not be satisfied if there is inadequacy, vagueness and inconsistency in the statement of reasons. Another essential procedural requirement is that of consultation where so required. In the *Isoglucose* cases, 138 and 139/79 [1980] ECR 3333, the Court struck down a Regulation on the grounds of the Council's failure to obtain the opinion of the European Parliament.

3. Infringement of the Treaty or any rule of law relating to its application

This is a very important ground of review. The first two grounds seem to be subsumed under this head, and this ground is pleaded in virtually all annulment actions. It seems to be wider than any comparable rule under English law, and includes breach of any general principles of law, such as equality or proportionality, as well as violation of human rights.

4. Misuse of power

This involves an illegitimate use of power on the part of the institution concerned. This is a difficult ground to establish, and there is very little case law, as far as the EEC Treaty is concerned.

There is much overlap among these grounds, and the Court does not always clarify the exact ground which forms the basis of its decision.

Where an annulment action under Article 173 proves successful, the European Court will declare the act void under Article 174, although it also has the power to declare a measure void in part only.

Review of Community inaction – Article 175

Sometimes, inactivity on the part of Community institutions can be as damaging as wrongful action. The party complaining about this inaction may be another Community institution. In case 13/83 *European*

Parliament v *Council* [1986] 1 CMLR 138, the European Parliament brought an action against the Council, alleging its failure to implement a common transport policy, as the European Parliament alleged it was obliged to do under the EEC Treaty. Or it may be a private individual or corporation that is seeking to compel the Community to do something, such as taking action against infringements of Community competition or anti-dumping law.

Article 175 permits review of failure to act by the Council and Commission. The first paragraph of Article 175 states: "Should the Council or Commission, in infringement of this Treaty, fail to act, the Member States and the other institutions of the Community may bring an action before the Court of Justice to have the infringement established."

The applicant must show that the institution's failure to act is "in infringement of the Treaty". This must be a violation of a provision which imposes an obligation to act – a mere discretionary power (such as the right of the Commission to commence proceedings against Member States under Article 169 for their failure to fulfil their obligations under the Treaty) is not sufficient. Failure to take non-binding acts is expressly excluded from the remit of Article 175, as they are under Article 173.

In case 15/70 *Chevalley* v *Commission* [1970] ECR 975, the European Court held that Articles 173 and 175 "merely provide one and the same method of recourse". This is now known as the "unity principle" and has the important consequence that any inconsistencies between the two remedies should be resolved by applying the same principles to both. Thus the unity principle would suggest that Article 175 is concerned only with the failure to issue a binding act, as only binding acts may be reviewed under Article 173. Likewise, although inaction on the part of the Parliament is not included in the wording of Article 175, it would now seem that since the Parliament can be subject to Article 173 proceedings, it should also be subject to proceedings taken under Article 175.

Locus standi

All Member States have privileged status, as do *all* three Community institutions, including the European Parliament, which in 1985 brought a successful action against the Commission and Council, for the failure to issue a common transport policy (see above). Such privileged applicants can challenge any failure to adopt any binding act which it is the institutions' duty to adopt.

Natural or legal persons may only bring proceedings where the institution has failed to address to that person an act other than a recommendation or opinion (Art 175, para 3). It seems that an individual is only likely to be successful in complaining of a failure to act in circumstances in which, had the Institution acted, the act would have been of direct and individual concern to the complainant. In Case 246/81 *Lord Bethell* v *Commission* [1982] ECR 2277, the applicant (a member of the "freedom of the skies" campaign) sought to force the Commission to take action under Article 89 against Member States' airlines for their allegedly anti-competitive practices. The European Court rejected his application, on the basis that there was no failure to adopt a measure that he was legally entitled to claim. It seems clear that Article 175 cannot be used to circumvent the restricted rights of direct access to judicial review under Article 173, by arguing that *e.g.* the Commission has "failed to act" because it has not acted in a way the complainant wishes, by *e.g.* refusing his application for a licence.

Procedure

Before an action for failure to act can be lodged, the institution concerned must be called upon to act (Art 175, para 2). The institution then has two months to take the requested act, or to "define its position", which means a clear statement either accepting or rejecting the request to act. If the institution defines its position, proceedings under Article 175 come to an end (although proceedings under Article 173 may still be possible). If, however, the institution does nothing, the applicant has two months to bring the case before the European Court.

If the applicant succeeds with his action, the institution will be required to remedy its failure and to "take the necessary steps to comply with the judgment of the European Court" (Art 176). However, there are no further sanctions in the event of non-compliance (except the possibility of another action under Art 175.).

Plea of illegality

Article 184 provides another means of challenging the legality of Community action – in this case Regulations, providing that certain conditions are satisfied. Article 184 states:

> "Notwithstanding the expiry of the period laid down in the third paragraph of Article 173, any party may, in proceedings in which a Regulation of the Council or Commission is in issue, plead the grounds specified in the first paragraph of Article 173, in order to invoke before the Court of Justice the inapplicability of this Regulation."

But although Article 184 allows individuals to challenge Regulations (which they cannot generally do) they may only do so where the Regulation is put in issue in the course of proceedings which have already begun in the European Court. The challenge is an indirect one. It does not provide a means of bringing the action to court for the first time. Thus, for example, if an individual is challenging the legality of a decision addressed to him by the Commission, Article 184 enables him to challenge the legality of the Regulation on which the decision was based.

Actions against the Community for damages for non-contractual liability

Judicial review by the European Court provides a means of ensuring that the Community institutions do not exceed or misuse the powers allotted to them. However, review, and even the subsequent declaration of nullity of the act concerned, may not provide an adequate remedy for an applicant who has suffered great loss as a result of wrongful action by a Community institution. The applicant may, however, be able to recover damages from the Community for that loss.

Community liability in tort (non-contractual liability) is governed by Articles 178 and 215(2). Article 178 provides:

> "The Court of Justice shall have jurisdiction in disputes relating to the compensation for damage provided for in the second paragraph of Article 215."

Article 215(2) provides:

> "In the case of non-contractual liability, the Community shall, in accordance with the general principles common to the laws of the Member States, make good any damage caused by its institutions or by its servants in the performance of their duties."

There is no definition of the concept of a wrongful act in Community law. However, on the basis of general principles common to the laws of the Member States the European Court requires:
1. a fault committed by the Community, either by its Institutions (a *faute de service*) or by its servants (a *faute personelle*).
2. damage suffered by the applicant.
3. a causal link between the two.

The range of wrongful acts that may be committed by the Community is wide. It includes a physical act, such as driving a motor car and causing physical injuries; the failure to correct misleading information, and anything else capable of causing harm to others. In Case 145/83 *Adams v Commission* [1985] ECR 3539, the European Court held that the Commission had violated a duty of confidence owed to the applicant under EC competition law. Adams, a former employee of the Swiss firm, Hoffman-La Roche, after requesting confidentiality, had given the Commission documents, indicating that the company was violating EC competition law. The Commission then brought proceedings against Hoffman-La Roche, as a result of which it was fined. However, in the course of these proceedings, the Commission breached the duty of confidentiality owed to Adams, partly by failing to warn him that Hoffman-La Roche was planning to have him prosecuted under Swiss law. As a result, Adams was in fact charged and kept in solitary confinement, convicted of industrial espionage and suffered irreparable financial and emotional damage. Adams was one of the few applicants who succeeded in recovering damages against the Commission in the European Court (although reduced by half for contributory negligence).

The wrongful act may also be legislative in nature, causing damage by its legal effects. A very important body of case law concerns complaints arising from the effects of Community legislation, *e.g.* where the applicant suffers loss as a result of a Regulation which he claims is discriminatory or illegal in some way.

Initially, it seemed that an action first had to be brought to annul the act concerned (under Art 173) before proceedings to recover damages could succeed. This was the view taken by the Court in Case 25/62 *Plaumann* [1963] ECR 95, which held that "An administrative measure which has not been annulled cannot of itself constitute a wrongful act on the part of the administration inflicting damage upon those whom it affects." However, in its later case law the European Court relaxed this requirement, stressing that actions for damages and actions for annulment are distinct and different actions. In Case 4/69 *Lütticke* [1971] ECR at 336 the Court stated that "The action for damages provides for by Article 178 and the second paragraph of Article 215 was established by the Treaty as an independent form of action with a particular purpose to fulfil within the system of actions."

Where the alleged wrongful act is individual in nature, the applicant will find it easier to claim damages than where the act is normative, involving the exercise of discretion on the part of the Community institution concerned. Acts of the former sort only affect the addressee (if a decision) or the person unlucky enough to suffer its consequences. However, legislative acts such as Regulations can affect a wide group of people, and Community business would become unworkable if they were easily challenged in the course of actions for damages.

Thus, the requirements that must be satisfied by an applicant seeking damages for loss caused by an act of a legislative nature are very strict. It is not sufficient to show that the act in question is unlawful, nor that a Community institution had unlawfully failed to act. In fact, in Case 5/71 *Zuckerfabrik Schöppenstedt* [1971] ECR at 984, the Court held:

> "Where a legislative measure involving choices of economic policy is concerned, the Community does not incur non-contractual liability for damage suffered by individuals as a consequence of that action, by virtue of the provisions contained in the second paragraph of Article 215, unless a sufficiently flagrant violation of a superior rule of law for the protection of the individual has occurred."

This is known as the "Schöppenstedt" formula. It has three elements.

1. It concerns only legislative acts which involve choices of economic policy.

    Although such legislative acts are primarily Regulations, the term also covers any general act laying down binding rules which apply to an indefinite category of persons. The act must also involve "choices of economic policy". Most legislative acts involve such choices, since the institutions have wide discretionary powers, and most measures, even those involving social policy, can be construed as economic, since the EEC Treaty is an economic one.

2. A breach of a superior rule of law for the protection of individuals.

   It seems that most of the principles established by the EEC Treaty would count as superior rules of law – *e.g.* free movement of goods and workers, as well as general principles of law such as proportionality or equality. The rule must also be for the protection of individuals. However, this test will be satisfied if the rule is intended to protect interests of a general nature, providing this includes the interests of the applicant.

3. The breach must be "sufficiently serious".

   The fact that there are grounds to annul an act (or even that the act complained of *has* been annulled) does not mean that damages will be awared. The Community must be guilty of a "sufficiently serious" breach. This requirement has been interpreted very restrictively.

In Cases 83, 94/76, 4, 15, 40/77 *Bayerische HNL* [1978] ECR 1209 the Court stated that the Community will not be liable for damage unless the institution concerned has "manifestly and gravely disregarded the limits of the exercise of its powers". This action had arisen as a result of Community action to get rid of the skimmed-milk powder mountain. A Regulation had been passed requiring animal feed producers to purchase skimmed-milk powder instead of the cheaper soya as a source of animal feed. The farmers objected, as they had to pay more for their animal feed and actions were brought to contest the legality of the regulation, which was ruled invalid in the course of Article 177 proceedings, for offending the principles of discrimination and proportionality (in Cases 114/76 116/76 *Bela-Mühle* and *Granaria* [1977] ECR 1247).

However, the Court held that the breach was not "sufficiently serious" in order for the applicants to recover damages in tort proceedings – the violation was not, in the European Court's words "manifest and grave". It affected a wide group of persons, the price increase had only a limited effect on production costs, insignificant when compared to increases caused by fluctuations in world prices, and the effect of the regulation on their profits did not exceed the normal level of risk inherent in such activities.

In contrast, in the *Quellmehl* and *Gritz* cases [1979] ECR 2955, the Court did award damages for severe losses suffered as result of a Council decision to withdraw subsidies from producers of quellmehl and gritz (peculiar substances, used in baking and brewing) while retaining them for starch, a product with which they were in competition. The European Court had earlier struck down the decision (in an Article 177 reference) on the grounds that it was discriminatory. In this case, the Court held that the applicants were a small, clearly defined group, and that their losses went beyond those inherent in business.

However, two months later in the *Isoglucose* cases (143/77, 116 & 124/77 [1979] ECR 3497, 3583) the Court took a different approach. The applicants were isoglucose producers, a product in competition with sugar, who sought damages for losses suffered when Community Regulations removed subsidies and imposed large levies on isoglucose to protect sugar production. Losses of up to £30 million were suffered by isoglucose producers, who were able to have the regulations struck down (in an Article 177 reference) as infringing the principle of equality. The applicants were a small, closed group, who suffered terrific losses. Following the *Quellmehl* and *Gritz* cases one might have thought they would succeed in recovering damages. However, the European Court was concerned, not with the extent of the harm, but the conduct of the Community institution – holding that the Community would only be liable if its conduct were "verging on the arbitrary".

Thus it seems that applicants must show both that the scale of the loss *and* the Community's violation of the law is manifest and grave if he is to succeed. This is unfortunate, for it may mean that an applicant, who has suffered severe losses as a result of Community action, may be left without a remedy, or compensation.

Concurrent liability

The difficulty of bringing successful proceedings in the European Court may mean that the applicant seeks to proceed instead in his own national courts. However, to do so, he must first find a cause of action under EC law that raises a question of EEC law. This is not always possible. Where he is able to do so, he may be able to raise the point of EC law before the national courts, and seek a reference to the European Court under Article 177, to determine its validity. However, the national courts have no jurisdiction to award damages for wrongful acts specifically attributable to the *Community*. But as much of Community law is implemented by national authorities, actions for damages may sometimes be brought against them. The case law is not very clear, but it seems that claims for sums unlawfully paid to national authorities should be brought in the national courts, whereas claims for unliquidated damages as a result of illegal Community action can only be brought before the European Court. Either way, it is suggested that the applicant will find it very difficult to recover anything. Successful actions for damages brought against the Community are the exception rather than the rule.

Community law in the national court

Fergus Randolph in his contribution considered some of the issues involved in the applying Community law in the national courts and in particular the issues arising out of *Factortame* and the Sunday trading cases. Between 1974 and 1989 there were 65 judgments arising out of the use of Article 177 covering very important matters such as immigration policy in Case 41/74 *Van Duyn* v *Home Office*, trade mark rights in Case 51/75 *EMI* v *CBS* and sex discrimination in Case 129/79 *McCarthys Ltd* v *Wendy Smith* (129/79).

The issue of prohibition of Sunday trading and compatibility with the Treaty has recently been the subject of an Article 177 reference to the European Court of Justice by the Magistrates Court in Cwmbran in Case 145/88 *Torfaen Borough Council* v *B & B plc*, who asked the following questions:

(1) "Where a Member State prohibits retail premises from being open on a Sunday for the sale of goods to customers, save in respect of certain specified items, sales of which are permitted, and where the effect of the prohibition is to reduce in absolute terms the sales of goods in those premises, including goods manufactured in other Member States, and correspondingly to reduce the volume of imports of goods from other Member States, is such a prohibition a measure having equivalent effect to a quantitative restriction on imports within the meaning of Article 30 of the Treaty?"

(2) "If the answer to Question 1 is in the affirmative, does such a measure benefit from any of the exceptions to Article 30 contained in Article 36, or from any other exception recognised by Community law?"

(3) "Is the answer to Question 1 or Question 2 above affected by any other factor so as to render the measure in question a means of arbitrary discrim-

ination or a disguised restriction on trade between Member States or a measure is lacking in proportionality or otherwise unjustified?"

The European Court of Justice replied that Article 30 of the Treaty:

"Must be interpreted as meaning that the prohibition which it lays down does not apply to national rules prohibiting retailers from opening their premises on Sunday where the restrictive effects on Community trade which may result therefrom do not exceed the effects intrinsic to rules of that kind. In the light of the reply given to the first question, it is unnecessary to answer the second and third questions."

The problem remains as to how this somewhat equivocal ruling can be given effect in the United Kingdom and whether in fact section 47 of the Shops Act which prohibits Sunday trading can remain.

Another important use of an Article 177 reference was in Case 213/89 *R* v *Secretary of State for Transport ex parte Factortame Ltd and others*. In this case the House of Lords asked the European Court of Justice:

(1) "Where (i) a party before the national court claims to be entitled to rights under Community law having direct effect in national law ['the rights claimed'], (ii) a national measure in clear terms will, if applied, automatically deprive that party of the rights claimed, (iii) there are serious arguments both for and against the existence of the rights claimed and the national courlt has sought a preliminary ruling under Article 177 as to whether or not the rights claimed exist, (iv) the national law presumes the national measure in question to be compatible with Community law until it is declared incompatible, (v) the national court has no power to give interim protection to the rights claimed by suspending the application of the national measure pending the preliminary ruling, (vi) if the preliminary ruling is in the event in favour of the rights claimed, the party entitled to those rights is likely to have suffered irremediable damage unless given such interim protection, does Community Law either (a) oblige the national court to grant such interim protection of the rights claimed; or (b) give the court power to grant such interim protection of the rights claimed?"

(2) If question 1(a) is answered in the negative and question 1(b) in the affirmative, what are the criteria to be applied in deciding whether or not to grant such interim protection of the rights claimed?"

The European Court of Justice replied that where the sole obstacle to granting interim relief is a rule of national law then that rule must be set aside – a judgment which has important ramifications for the granting of interim measures by national courts.

These are but two recent examples of important decisions handed down by the Court by way of an Article 177 reference. Others include the case of *Foster* v *British Gas* (Case 188/89). What there does appear to be is a growing trend of greater willingness to refer cases to the European Court of Justice. Furthermore, the growing effect of Community law within the UK legal system can no longer be brushed aside. This increasing impact is reflected in, for example, Mustill LJ's speech in *WH Smith Do-It-All* v *Peterborough City Council* [1990] 2 CMLR 577 where he states that:

> "If Parliament speaks, the court must obey. This is still the fundamental principle of our constitutional law, but it has more recently been overlaid with qualifications of increasing importance to daily life stemming from the accession of the United Kingdom to the European Communities. Since then the courts have been obliged to read statutes of the United Kingdom in the light of the general principles laid down in the Treaty of Rome, as developed in instruments of the Council and Commission, and as expounded by the European Court of Justice."

European Court of Justice breaking new ground

John Usher's chapter is an analysis of the extent to which the Court of Justice has moved beyond the express jurisdiction conferred on it by the Treaty. He explores this proposition through an assessment of the Court's handling of:
–acts susceptible to annulment,
–actions taken by the European Parliament, and,
–precedent.

Acts susceptible to annulment

In this section of his paper Usher focuses on judicial control of non-binding acts which, although they may not be challenged, still have important legal effects. Such judicial control as there is has been developed through the case law starting with *Usines à Tubes de la Sarre*. In that case it was held that where a reasoned opinion is required, and not given, the defect is of such a nature as to suggest that the act did not exist within the meaning of Article 54 of the ECSC Treaty. In other words, what the Court is doing is equating a declaration of inexistence to the more usual remedy of a declaration of nullity.

An extension of this notion came with the famous case of *"Les Verts"* v *European Parliament* in which the French Greens challenged some decisions of the Parliament concerning appropriations granted as a contribution to the information campaign of the elections to the Parliament. An action was brought under Article 173 of the Treaty which speaks only of acts of the Council and Commission. The Court held that the general scheme of the Treaty could be interpreted to be deemed to take full account of all measures adopted by any institutions so long as these measures produced legal effects.

The mere fact that the Parliament was not mentioned in Article 173 can be explained in the context of the role of the Parliament envisaged at the time of drafting the Treaty. Originally it was perceived that the Parliament's powers would amount to limited political control and mere consultation. The fact that Parliament's acts could produce legal effects in relation to third parties is a relatively recent phenomenon. Furthermore, given that there is only one provision in the Treaty for annulment of acts of the institutions, it must, in the light of the spirit of the Treaty, be construed to incorporate acts of the Parliament. Any other interpretation would also be flawed for being illogical on the grounds that it would exclude from review acts of the Parliament thereby creating a loophole for Member States to trespass powers of the Parliament or allow the Parliament to act *ultra vires* and not be accountable. The author sees this as effectively re-writing Article 173 to ensure a comprehensive system of judicial control of acts of the Community institutions in relation to third parties.

Actions by the European Parliament

The Parliament has been trying to gain *locus standi* in order to bring actions for annulment against measures adopted by the Council and Commission. Article 173 expressly restricts actions of this sort to the Council and the Commission. This narrow interpretation of action for annulment is further reinforced by similar rules laid down in Articles 33 and 38 of the ECSC Treaty.

Usher traces this attempt to gain *locus standi* in the face of a lack of Treaty support to Case 302/87 *European Parliament* v *Council* where the Parliament actually brought a direct action for annulment. The Court rejected the proposition on the grounds that the remedies available to the Parliament lay in the political sphere and that the more appropriate course of action would have been to ask the Commission to bring an action on behalf of the Parliament.

However, a shift in this stance was pronounced in the later case of *European Parliament* v *Council* (Case 70/88) which concerned legislation governing the maximum levels of radioactive contamination for foodstuffs following a nuclear accident. Although the litigants were the Parliament and the Council, in reality the Parliament was challenging the notion that the Commission could be relied upon to act on its behalf to challenge proposed legislation which the Commission itself had drafted and based on what the Parliament believed to be the wrong Treaty basis.

In this instance the Court of Justice found that there may be circumstances where, although the Commission is required to ensure the prerogatives of the Parliament are observed, they could not be expected to require the Commission to bring an action which it itself believed to be ill-conceived. As such, the Court concluded that to protect the prerogatives of the Parliament and to ensure respect for the powers of the institutions, it was necessary that there should be a judicial remedy available to ensure respect for the Parliament's prerogatives.

Yet the dilemma for the Court was how to achieve this respect for the Parliament's prerogatives while simultaneously preventing the Parliament from having the same status of privileged litigants enjoyed by both the Council and the Commission. A judicial compromise was reached which Usher rightly assesses as an effectively new version of the action for annulment applicable only to the Parliament. Under this re-written action for annulment, the Parliament could bring an action for annulment against other institutions provided the action was intended to safeguard the Parliament's prerogatives and that it was based on grounds related to the violation of these prerogatives. The author does, however, point out that while this may be a new version for an action for annulment, it does shadow similar developments in resolving the conflicts involved in determining direct and individual concern mentioned earlier in this introduction.

Precedent

European lawyers are by now familiar with the Court's citation of its previous decisions when following them on the one hand and its notorious reluctance on the other hand to state directly when it is not following earlier caselaw. However, in the recent case of *Parliament* v *Council* (1990) an interesting feature was that for the first time the Court expressly referred to an earlier judgment, examining in detail its reasoning, and then concluding that the remedies it had then suggested were actually not sufficiently effective or certain. This allowed the Court to reach a different conclusion that was an express departure from its earlier decision. Such a novel approach by the Court has been repeated in the recent decision of Case C-10/89 *CNL-SUCAL* v *HAG* concerning the doctrine of common origin. The Court is thus appearing to move to the position where it no longer simply treats earlier case law as a reference point to save it giving detailed reasoning in later cases, but rather using precedent as a sufficiently important source of law for the Court to state expressly when it is not following it.

New general jurisdiction?

So far we have looked at the development of new versions of old remedies. Usher believes, however, that we may be moving into uncharted territory involving a general jurisdiction of the Court of Justice not envisaged by those drafting the Treaty. Such a new jurisdiction is asserted on the basis of general Treaty provisions as was done in Case C-2/88 *IMM Zwartveld*. In that case the Dutch judge wanted to investigate alleged fraud of the Community fishing quota and claimed that he was unable to proceed unless he had access to certain reports prepared by Commission officials. He also wanted Commission officials to give evidence before him.

The Commission objected to this on a number of grounds believing that that the proper way to proceed was through an Article 177 reference which, in this instance, was not even available since the Dutch judge did not want the interpretation of a provision of Community law.

The Court's response was to invite submissions from both the Community institutions and the Member States and a considerable amount of interest was stirred up. The reasoning of the Court emphasised the duty of loyal co-operation as stated in Article 5 of the Treaty and its requirement of observation of reciprocal duties of loyal co-operation with Member States. Indeed, Community institutions were duty-bound to ensure that Treaty provisions were applied. In the light of this duty they were required to give active support to the national judge by giving documentation and allowing Commission officials to give evidence.

The Court also invoked Article 164 which creates a duty to ensure that in the interpretation and application of the Treaty the law is observed. Given Article 164, the Court held that it was seized of the case and could claim jurisdiction to determine in this case whether refusal to co-operate by the institutions was justified in the light of the need to avoid interference with their proper functioning.

In other words, the Court allowed itself a new judicial remedy which extended its jurisdiction by reference to two general articles of the Treaty, namely Articles 5 and 164. The author also shows that this technique is one the Court may have adapted from the Commission who similarly gave itself jurisdiction on the basis of Articles 5 and 155 in an agricultural matter. The door appears according to Usher to have opened "to new sorts of judicial control in the complex relationship between the institutions and the Member States".

Court of First Instance of the European Communities

Tim Millet's chapter mentioned earlier explores the detailed workings of the new Court of First Instance. Given that in excess of 600 cases are currently pending before the Court of Justice, it was inevitable that some structural change had to be made to decrease the workload of the Court. Indeed by 1988 the waiting period for a direct action was approximately 24 months. Such delays affect not only the quality of justice parties receive but are also damaging to the credibility of the institution to develop the "new legal order" it has sought. An added impetus for the setting up of the Court of First Instance naturally arises from the 1992 programme for the completion of the internal market.

Before attempting the creation of a new tier to the Court of Justice, several other methods for coping with the caseload of the Court had been tried. There had been an increase in staff but this growth had not been in line with the amount of work facing the Court. The Court also tried enforcing very stringent time limits on hearings. Furthermore, the Court conducted less plenary sessions preferring to dispose of cases through the use of five judge chambers. None of these solutions appeared to successfully tackle the growing backlog of cases and so a new court designed to hear mainly competition and staff matters was created.

Although the Court of First Instance was only set up in 1989, agreement on the principle of such an institution dates back to 1974 when the Council of Ministers expressed agreement on the need for a first instance court to hear disputes between the Community institutions and its servants. Yet it was not until the Single European Act (OJ 1987 L169) that a new Article 168A and a new second paragraph to Article 188 of the EEC Treaty, was introduced which established the framework for the Court of First Instance.

Article 188 as amended allowed the Council to amend the provisions of Title III of the Statute of the Court of Justice entitled "Procedure". The new Article 168A provides for the actual establishment of the Court of First Instance. It provides that:

> "At the request of the Court of Justice and after consulting the Commission and the European Parliament, the Council may, acting unanimously, attach to the Court of Justice a court with jurisdiction to hear and determine at first instance, subject to a right of appeal to the Court of Justice on points of law only and in accordance with the conditions laid down by the Statute, certain clauses of action or proceeding brought by natural or legal persons. That court shall not be competent to hear and determine actions brought by Member States or by Community Institutions or questions referred for a preliminary ruling under Article 177."

in other words, the Court of First Instance is not a new, independent court but a body attached to the Court of Justice with its seat in Luxembourg.

Since Millet's article was submitted the Rules of Procedure have been published (OJ 1991 L136/1) and this introduction takes account of the Rules. The Rules are set out in the Appendix to this book.

Composition and organization

The Court of First Instance consists of 12 members appointed by common accord who sit for six-yearly terms. While nationality is not a consideration in the appointment of judges, the present composition of the Court of First Instance includes a representative of each of the Member States. The Court also has a President who would normally be chosen by the other members of the Court. However, the first president was appointed by common accord of the governments. Half the members of the Court of First Instance are replaced every three years and this is done by lot by the President of the Council of Ministers.

While there are no Advocates-General the Council Decision (88/591/ECSC, EEC, Euratom) establishing the Court of First Instance provides that members may be called upon to act as Advocates-General. According to Article 17 of the Rules of Procedure the Court must be assisted by an Advocate-General whenever there is a plenary session. Article 18 also states that an Advocate-General may be used where "the legal difficulties or the factual complexity of the case so requires". The decision to designate an Advocate-General is one that must be taken by a plenary session of the Court and the actual designation decided by the President.

Article 2(4) of the above Council Decision also states that this Court *shall* sit in chambers of three or five judges but that it may in certain circumstances, sit in plenary session. A plenary session would be one with a quorum of seven judges. It is possible to have a plenary session at *any* stage in the proceedings either at the initiative of the chambers hearing the case or at the request of one of the parties. A plenary session of the Court would determine whether the case should be so referred to a plenary Court.

Additionally, since the Court of First Instance is attached to the Court and not a separate institution, it uses the translation, library and research facilities of the Court. It does however have its own Registrar and each judge has a small personal staff.

Jurisdiction

The jurisdiction of the Court falls into four main categories. All staff cases are now heard before this Court. The new Court also hears actions for annulment or actions for failure to act brought by undertakings or by associations of undertakings against the Commission concerning individual acts relating to the application of Articles 50 and

57–66 of the ECSC Treaty. A third category of cases now within the jurisdiction of this Court is that of actions for annulment or actions for failure to act brought by natural or legal persons against an institution of the Communities relating to the implementation of the competition rules applicable to undertakings under the EEC Treaty. The final class of cases that may be brought before this Court is that of a claim for damages brought by a natural or legal person where the damage is alleged to arise from an act or a failure to act which is the subject of an action under one of the heads previously listed. Eventually the Court of First Instance will also handle all anti-dumping matters but Article 3(3) of the Council Decision does not envisage this happening until late 1991.

It is clear that moving staff cases to the Court of First Instance (which accounts for 20–25% of the litigation before the Court) was a useful method of lightening the Court's workload. The disputes are usually concerned with terms of employment and are not a direct concern of the law on European integration.

The major jurisprudence of the Court of First Instance will however come from its decisions in competition cases. The extent to which this jurisprudence develops depends on whether these decisions go on appeal to the Court. Further, the Court still retains control over competition matters which come to it by way of a reference for a preliminary ruling.

In circumscribing the jurisdiction of the Court of First Instance two major possible areas of jurisdiction have been excluded. The first omission is for actions relating to state aids brought by natural or legal persons. Cases brought by natural or legal persons under an arbitration clause pursuant to Article 181 of the EEC Treaty have also been excluded from the ambit of the Court of First Instance's jurisdiction. It is hoped that these could be successfully included at a later date when the new court is well established.

Procedure

Agreement on the new Court's Rules of Procedure has only recently been reached as indicated earlier. From the Single European Act we already knew that certain differences in procedure would apply. While the Advocate-General's opinion before the European Court must be read in open court, the Advocate-General before the Court of First Instance may deliver his opinion in writing.

Where a procedural document is lodged with the wrong registry the new Statute governing the European Court states that it should be "immediately" transferred to the right registry. In instances where a court finds that it docs not have jurisdiction it may refer the case to the other court. There are also rules governing conflicts where each court has jurisdiction over a case but the case raises the same issue.

The Court of First Instance enjoys the same powers to order interim measures as the European Court. Its judgments take effect and have the same limitations as a judgment of the European Court. Final decisions of the Court of First Instance are notified by the Registrar to the parties concerned, Member States and Community institutions (even where they are not parties to the action).

Appeal to the Court of Justice

Article 51 of the Statute of the European Court states that decisions of the Court of First Instance are subject to appeal on points of law only. Such an appeal may be on one of three grounds. An appeal may be based on a lack of competence of the Court of First Instance. There may be an appeal for breach of procedure before the new court. Appeal is also possible against any infringement of Community law by the Court of First Instance. Normally, such appeals must be brought within two months of notification of the decision unless it is an appeal against a decision to intervene in proceedings before the Court of First Instance in which case the appeal must be within two weeks of the date of notification.

Any appeals against decisions of the Court of First Instance may be lodged with the Registry of either the European Court or the Court of First Instance and drafted in the language of the case before the Court of First Instance. It is possible to amend one's appeal if there is a procedural inconsistency so long as this is done within a reasonable time of lodging the appeal.

Where a Member State or Community institution wishes to intervene at this stage of the proceedings although they were not present at the proceedings before the Court of First Instance, they may place an application to this effect within three months of the date the appeal was lodged.

One departure from the normal procedure in cases of an appeal from the Court of First Instance is that the Court may, if it so chooses, dispense with an oral hearing. However there can be no dispensation where a party object on the grounds that the written phase did not allow him to put forward his case fully.

In instances of appeals against interim orders of the Court of First Instance the President of the European Court may decide the matter by way of summary procedure.

*Sionaidh Douglas-Scott and Ingrid Persaud, King's College London

Chapter 2

Reference to the European Court of Justice under Article 177*

Jurisdiction of European Court of Justice under Article 177

Article 177 of the EEC Treaty provides a mechanism whereby the domestic courts of Member States may refer problems of EC law to the European Court of Justice in Luxembourg. The full text of Article 177 is as follows:

"The Court of Justice shall have jurisdiction to give preliminary rulings concerning:
(a) the interpretation of this Treaty;
(b) the validity and interpretation of acts of the institutions of the Community;
(c) the interpretation of the statutes of bodies established by an act of the Council, where those statutes so provide.

Where such a question is raised before any court or tribunal of a Member State, that court of tribunal may, if it considers that a decision on the question is necessary to enable it to give judgment, request the Court of Justice to give a ruling thereon.

Where any such question is raised in a case pending before a court of tribunal of a Member State, against whose decision there is no judicial remedy under national law, that court or tribunal shall bring the matter before the Court of Justice."

Similar provisions are to be found in Article 150 of the Euratom Treaty and in Article 14 of the ECSC Treaty; also in the Protocol to the 1968 Brussels Convention on Jurisdiction and the Enforcement of Judgments in Civil and Commercial Matters (see the Civil Jurisdiction and Judgments Act 1982) and the Protocol to the 1980 Rome Convention on Contractual Obligations (see the Contracts (Applicable Law) Act 1990).

Several general points on the Article 177 procedure require emphasis.

Underlying purpose – the achievement of uniformity and harmonization

The underlying purpose of Article 177 is to achieve uniformity and harmonization in the application of Community law in all 12 Member States. The Court of Justice is, of course, in a unique position to comment on Community law. As Bingham J said in *Customs and Excise Commissioners* v *ApS Samex* [1983] 1 All ER 1042:

> "[The Court of Justice] has a panoramic view of the Community and its institutions, a detailed knowledge of the Treaties and of much subordinate legislation made under them, and an intimate familiarity with the functioning of the Community which no national judge denied the collective experience of the Court of Justice could hope to achieve".

Validity and interpretation

The Article 177 procedure can be used to determine both *validity* and *interpretation*. In practice references on the interpretation of legislation are much more common than references on validity. On validity it is important to note Case 314/85 *Firma Foto-Frost* v *Hauptzollamt Lübeck-Ost* [1988] 3 CMLR 57, in which the Court of Justice held that national authorities have a discretion whether or not to make a reference as to the validity of Community acts; however, they do not themselves have power to make a finding of *invalidity* of an act of the Community institutions: only the Court of Justice is able to declare such acts invalid. Domestic courts may, however, make *interim* orders suspending an administrative act of a national authority which is itself based upon a Community measure whose validity is in doubt, provided that the national court proceeds on the same basis as the Community Court in interim measure proceedings: Cases C-143/88 etc. *Zuckerfabrik Süderithmarschen AG* v *Hauptzollamt Itzehoe, The Times,* 27 March 1991.

Co-operative nature of the procedure

The Article 177 procedure is preliminary and co-operative, the co-operation being between the referring court and the Court of Justice. A reference to Luxembourg is not a contentious step in the proceedings; nor is it an "appeal" against the decision of a domestic court or tribunal

Court or tribunal

The meaning of "court or tribunal" in Article 177 is a matter of Community and not of domestic law. It is important to note that many specialist tribunals are able to make references. The Social Security Commissioner, the Special Commissioners for Income Tax and the VAT Tribunal have all made references under Article 177 from the United Kingdom. Essentially, the critical question is whether the "court or tribunal" is of a judicial nature. Where a government minister appoints its members, it is a permanent body charged with the settlement of disputes and is required to apply rules, this test is likely to be satisfied. In Case 109/88 *Handels-OG Kontorfunktionaernes Forbund i Danmark* v *Dansk Arbejdsgiverforening ex p Danfoss A/S* [1991] 1 CMLR 8 the Court of Justice held that the Danish Industrial Arbitration Board, which deals with disputes between the parties to collective agreements, was a "court or tribunal": either party may bring a case before the Board irrespective of the other's objections, so that its jurisdiction does not depend on the parties' agreement; furthermore the composition of the Board was not within the parties' discretion. Arbitral tribunals do not have the power to make a reference, at least where private arbitrators are appointed pursuant to an agreement between the parties. However, leave to appeal against an arbitrator's decision may be allowed on a fairly flexible basis where issues of Community law are raised, in which case it will be possible for the court dealing with the appeal itself to make a reference under Article 177. An example of this is afforded by *Bulk Oil (Zug) AG* v *Sun International Ltd* [1984] 1 All ER 386, where the legality of the UK Government's boycott of selling oil to Israel under EC law arose in an arbitration. Leave to appeal the arbitrator's determination on this was granted.

Courts of final resort

Note that Article 177 itself makes a distinction between the obligations of courts of final resort and other courts to make references: this is considered further under Courts of final resort, below.

Genuine dispute

There must be a genuine dispute between the parties before an Article 177 reference can be made: in Case 104/79 *Foglia* v *Novello* [1980] ECR 745; [1981] 1 CMLR 585 Italian wine growers became involved in litigation which was really intended to test the legality under EEC law of French tax legislation. If the Court of Justice is not satisfied that there is a genuine dispute between the litigants, it may refuse to give a preliminary ruling: it is not prepared to give abstract advisory opinions.

Who makes the reference?

It must be emphasised that it is the *domestic court or tribunal* that makes the reference, and not the parties; the writer recalls being asked by a defending solicitor in an action in which the domestic court had decided to make a reference how he (the solicitor) should make the reference and what the time limits were. He was puzzled that the Supreme Court Practice could give him no guidance on this!

Teleological reasoning

It is necessary to appreciate the importance in Community law of teleological reasoning when problems of interpretation arise. Where a Treaty article or a piece of subordinate legislation is difficult to understand, it is legitimate to ask what the provision in question was designed to achieve, bearing in mind the underlying objectives of Community law. For example, Article 30 of the Treaty forbids *quantitative* restrictions on imports of goods; in *R* v *Henn and Darby* the question arose whether a total import ban in respect of pornographic materials infringed Article 30. The Court of Appeal thought not, as a total ban had no reference to quantities; the Court of Justice, however, held that, if a ban on specific quantities was prohibited, it followed *a fortiori* that a total ban must be: Case 34/79 [1979] ECR 3795; [1980] 1 CMLR 246. When the matter returned to the House of Lords, Lord Diplock said:

> "[this case] serves as a timely warning to English judges not to be too ready to hold that because the meaning of the English text (which is one of six of equal authority) seems plain to them no question of interpretation can be involved. It was for this reason that your Lordships thought it proper to submit to the European Court for a preliminary ruling on the question as to the interpretation of Article 30 which is set out hereafter: it was not through any doubts upon your Lordships part as to the answer that would be received".

Language

Note also the particular problems of language, revealed for example in Case C-372/88 *Milk Marketing Board of England and Wales* v *Cricket St Thomas Estate* [1990] 2 CMLR 800. This case dealt with the statutory purchasing monopoly of the Milk Marketing Board of England and Wales (MMB). Regulation 1421/78, amending Regulation 804/68, recognises the MMB's exclusive right to buy from milk producers the milk which they produce and market "without processing". The Cricket St Thomas Estate ceased to pay contributions to the MMB in 1984 as required by the Milk Marketing Scheme. When the Board brought an action to recover the sums due, the Estate claimed that the Board's exclusive right to buy milk within the meaning of Article 25(1)(a) of Regulation 804/68 did not extend to milk "pasteurised" by the producer, as pasteurised milk does not satisfy the expression "milk which they produce and market *without processing*". The issue for the Court of Justice was therefore the precise meaning of the expression "without processing"; essentially the issue was whether the word "processed" means merely treated or means converted into some different form. The Court looked at other language versions of the relevant Regulation and concluded that the expression must mean "not converted into another form". It followed that the Board did have the exclusive right to purchase pasteurised milk and that therefore it was entitled to insist on payments from the Estate; judgment to this effect was subsequently given in *Milk Marketing Board* v *Cricket St Thomas Estate* (QBD, *Financial Times*, 22 March 1991).

Courts of Final Resort – Whether to Refer

Courts of final resort have an obligation to refer points of Community law, whereas lower courts simply have a discretion whether to refer. Apart from the problem of determining what is meant by a Court of final resort (see below), three points should be considered.

Acte clair

A court of final resort is not under an obligation to make a reference where the principle of *acte clair* applies, that is to say that the point of EC law is clear and free from doubt or that the Court of Justice has already dealt with it: see Case 283/81 *CILFIT* [1982] ECR 3415; [1983] 1 CMLR 472. The Court said in *CILFIT*:

> ". . . the correct application of Community law may be so obvious as to leave no scope for any reasonable doubt as to the manner in which the question raised is to be resolved. Before it comes to the conclusion that such is the case, the national court or tribunal must be convinced that the matter is equally obvious to the courts of the other Member States and to the Court of Justice. Only if those conditions are satisfied may the national court or tribunal refrain from submitting the question to the Court of Justice and take upon itself the responsibility for resolving it".

Note, however, the points made above on the need for teleological reasoning and the problems of language that can arise in interpreting Community law. It is very important that judges in domestic courts interpret the Treaty in accordance with the principles of Community law.

Recent cases

There have been some extremely important recent references from the House of Lords under Article 177. Most noticeable of all was Case C-213/89 *R* v *Secretary of State for Transport, ex p Factortame Ltd* [1990] 3 CMLR 375 in which the Court of Justice held that any provisions of national law which might impair the effectiveness of Community law are incompatible with the obligations of Member States to ensure the legal protection that might be available to individuals under Community law. Following this judgment, the House of Lords itself granted an interim injunction restraining the UK Government from applying provisions of the Merchant Shipping Act 1988 in a way which might transgress Community law. In Case C-188/89 *Foster* v *British Gas plc* [1990] 2 CMLR 833 the Court of Justice had to consider whether female employees of British Gas, at the relevant time a statutory corporation, could rely on the Sex Discrimination Directive as against the defendant. The Court of Justice, consistently with earlier judgments, gave an answer sufficiently broad in its definition of the State to leave little doubt that they could so rely.

Refusal to refer

Clearly, a serious problem may occur if the court of final resort refuses to make a reference. The refusal of *lower* courts to refer may be appealed within the domestic legal system, but clearly this is not possible where there is no further domestic appeal. In this situation a Member State may itseslf be in breach of its obligations under the Treaty. The Commission could theoretically then bring proceedings under Article 169 against the Member State in question, although this would be likely to happen only in a very extreme case. The Commission would prefer to cajole the Member State into changing its ways without resort to proceedings.

Courts that are not of Final Resort – Whether to Refer

Where the court confronted with a problem of Community law is not a court of final resort, it is a matter of discretion whether a reference should be made. Five particular problems should be considered.

Is a decision necessary?

Article 177 says that a reference may be made "if [the court or tribunal] considers that a decision on the question is *necessary* to enable it to give judgment. . . ."

In *Bulmer* v *Bollinger* [1974] Ch 401 Lord Denning seemed to suggest that the expression "necessary" must mean that the point, whichever way decided, must be conclusive of the case. This is a very narrow formulation which has been disapproved on subsequent occasions (see for example *Polydor Limited* v *Harlequin Record Shops Limited* [1982] CMLR 413). In that case Ormrod LJ said that he "would regard the word 'necessary' as meaning 'reasonably necessary' in ordinary English and not 'unavoidable'."

The discretion

Lord Denning laid down some "Guidelines" in *Bulmer* v *Bollinger* [1974] Ch 401 as to how the discretion should be exercised. He mentioned the following factors:

(i)   the time it would take to obtain a ruling from the Court of Justice;
(ii) the importance of not overloading the Court of Justice;
(iii) the need to formulate the question clearly;
(iv) the difficulty and importance of the point;
(v)   the expense of getting a ruling;
(vi) the wishes of the parties.

There has been criticism that Lord Denning's guidelines are too restrictive and that the tenor of his judgment is to discourage lower courts from making references under Article 177. However, in subsequent cases lower courts have not been noticeably unwilling to refer points to the Court of Justice. If anything the *acte clair* doctrine seems to have acted as a prompt to domestic courts to make a reference to the Court of Justice. For example in *R* v *Pharmaceutical Society of Great Britain, ex parte the Association of Pharmaceutical Importers* [1987] 3 CMLR 951 Kerr LJ said that "our courts should hesitate long" before reaching a conclusion that the answer to a question of EEC Law was so obvious as to leave no room for any reasonable doubt. In *R* v *Secretary of State for Transport, ex parte Factortame Limited* the Divisional Court expressed a similar view, Hodgson J paraphrasing the words of the Court of Justice in *CILFIT* as follows:

> "speaking entirely for myself, I realise that I am not well qualified to 'place in its context every provision of Community law nor to interpret it in the light of Community law as a whole'."

As the list at the end of this paper shows, many cases have been referred from UK courts and tribunals.

Importance of establishing the relevant facts

In most of the references from the United Kingdom, the court in question did not make a reference until the relevant facts of the case had been established or unless there were no substantial disagreements between the parties as to the facts. A good example of the court's practice was *Lord Bethell* v *Sabena* [1983] 3 CMLR 1 where Parker J declined to make a reference in a case concerning the difficult question of the application of the competition rules in the Treaty to the air transport sector at a stage in the proceedings when the relevant facts had yet to be established.

Small sums of money

Small sums of money may involve large points of law; although it will often be inappropriate to make an expensive reference to Luxembourg in view of the small amount at stake, some important points of Community law have been established in just these circumstances. For example in Case 172/80 *Zuchner* v *Bayerische Vereinsbank AG* [1981] ECR 2021; [1982] 1 CMLR 313 a German plaintiff, concerned that he had been charged a fixed amount of commission for foreign currency transactions, brought an action against the defendant bank complaining that it was guilty of acting illegally under Article 85 of the Treaty. The sum in question was tiny, but on reference to the Court of Justice it was established that the competition rules in the Treaty apply as much to the banking sector as to any other part of the economy, a very important principle of Community law.

Appeals against a decision to refer/not to refer

Under Order 114 Rule 6 of the RSC, an Order making a reference to the Court of Justice under Article 177 is deemed to be a final order.

This means that an appeal against it lies to the Court of Appeal without leave. In a recent case in Scotland, *Procurator Fiscal, Elgin* v *Cowie* [1990] 3 CMLR 445 (Scottish High Court of Justiciary) the High Court concluded that it would not be justified in interfering with a lower court's exercise of its discretion to refer to the Court of Justice in Luxembourg unless they felt that its decision was plainly wrong. It is reasonable to expect that the appellate courts in England and Wales would adopt a similar attitude where a lower court has chosen to make a reference.

If a judge refuses to make a reference to the Court of Justice under Article 177, leave to appeal by the judge or the Court of Appeal is required because the decison is an interlocutory order.

What is meant by a Court of Final Resort?

There may be problems in determining whether a court or tribunal is a "court of final resort" for the purpose of Article 177(3). The problem arises in circumstances where there is no automatic right of appeal against a particular decision or judgment. For example, if the Court of Appeal refuses to give a litigant leave to appeal to the House of Lords and if the House of Lords refuses such leave, does this mean that the Court of Appeal in the particular proceedings was a "court of final resort"? If so it would have been bound under Article 177(3) to make a reference to Luxembourg in respect of any significant point of Community law. A point of this nature arose in *Magnavision NV* v *General Optical Council* [1987] 1 CMLR 887 in which the Divisional Court dismissed an appeal against conviction under the Opticians Act 1958. In doing so it rejected an argument that a prohibition on the selling of spectacles other than through a doctor or optician was contrary to Article 30 of the Treaty. The Divisional Court refused to certify that there was a point for consideration by the House of Lords. There is no appeal against a refusal by the Divisional Court to grant such a certificate in criminal proceedings. Subsequently, the Divisional Court refused to accept an argument that, by refusing such certification, it had become a court of final resort for the purposes of Article 177(3). The European Commission subsequently stated that it considered that the Divisional Court had denied the plaintiff an opportunity of having the question of Community law examined by a court of final instance which was bound by Article 177(3): see OJ 1988 C 310/44.

More recently *Generics (UK) Limited* v *Smith, Kline & French Laboratories Limited* [1990] 1 CMLR 416 was decided by the Court of Appeal. In a patent action, Generics (UK) Limited applied for a compulsory licence under Smith, Kline & French Laboratories Limited's ("SK&F") patent to manufacture, import and sell cimetidine and pharmaceutical formulations of it but could not agree on the terms. After the terms were settled by the Comptroller of Patents under section 46 of the Act, SK&F appealed to the Patents Court; both sides appealed its decision to the Court of Appeal

The Court took this opportunity to clarify its position concerning Article 177 and the court of last resort:

> "We are not, of course, the final appellate court for the purposes of Article 177 of the Treaty, even though an appeal to the House of Lords lies only with leave (citation omitted). So we are not *obliged* to refer the question to the EEC Court of Justice. But we have discretion."

In this particular case, the Court of Appeal did decided to make a reference, but it is significant that it did not consider itself bound to do so. A problem would arise if, in similar circumstances, courts decided not to refer to Luxembourg.

It is to be hoped that this particular conundrum will not give rise to serious problems in practice as a result of a willingness by lower courts to exercise their discretion in favour of Article 177 references.

Interlocutory Proceedings

References under Article 177 may be made in interlocutory proceedings. However, there is no obligation to refer, even on the part of a court of last resort, where an order for interim relief is made and can be reopened in subsequent proceedings.

The Reference

Order 114, Rule 1 RSC deals specifically with the procedure for making a reference under Article 177. In the case of County Courts, Rule 19(11) applies. Order 114 provides as follows:

Making of order

2(1). An order may be made by the Court of its own motion at any stage in a cause or matter, or on application by a party before or at the trial or hearing thereof.

2(2). Where an application is made before the trial or hearing, it shall be made by motion.

2(3). In the High Court no order shall be made except by a judge in person.

3. Schedule to order to set out request for ruling
An order shall set out in a schedule the request for the preliminary ruling of the European Court, and the Court may give directions as to the manner and form in which the schedule is to be prepared.

4. Stay of proceedings pending ruling
The proceedings in which an order is made shall, unless the Court otherwise orders, be stayed until the European Court has given a preliminary ruling of the question referred to it.

5. Transmission of order to the European Court
When an order has been made, the Senior Master shall send a copy thereof to the Registrar of the European Court; but in the case of an order made by the High Court, he shall not do so, unless the Court otherwise orders, until the time for appealing against the order has expired or, if an appeal is entered within that time, until the appeal has been determined of otherwise disposed of.

6. Appeals from orders made by the High Court
An order made by the High Court shall be deemed to be a final decision, and accordingly an appeal against it shall lie to the Court of Appeal without leave; but the period within which a notice of appeal must be served under Order 59, Rule 4(1), shall be 14 days.

Order 114, Rule 2 RSC:

[Heading as in cause or matter]
It is ordered that the question[s] set out in the Schedule hereto concerning the interpretation [or validity] of [specific Treaty provision or Community instrument or act concerned] be referred to the Court of Justice of the European Communities for a preliminary ruling in accordance with article 177 of the Treaty establishing the European Economic Community [or

article 150 of the Treaty establishing the European Atomic Energy Committee or article 41 of the Treaty establishing the European Coal and Steel Community or for a ruling under Schedule 2 to the Civil Jurisdiction and Judgments Act 1982, as the case may be].

And it is ordered that all further proceedings in the above-named cause [or matter] be stayed until the said Court of Justice has given its ruling on the said question[s] or until further order.

SCHEDULE
REQUEST FOR A PRELIMINARY RULING OF THE COURT OF JUSTICE OF THE EUROPEAN COMMUNITIES

(Here set out a clear and succinct statement of the case giving rise to the request for the ruling of the European Court of Justice in order to enable the European Court of Justice to consider and understand the issues of Community Law raised and to enable Governments of member states and other interested parties to submit observations. The statement of the case should include:

(a) particulars of the parties;
(b) the history of the dispute between the parties;
(c) the history of the proceedings;
(d) the relevant facts as agreed by the parties or found by the Court or, failing such agreement or finding, the contentions of the parties on such facts;
(e) the nature of the issues of law and fact between the parties;
(f) the (English) law, so far as is relevant, and
(g) the Treaty provisions or other Acts, Instruments or Rules of Community Law concerned.

The preliminary ruling of the Court of Justice of the European Communities is accordingly requested on the following questions: 1, 2 etc. (here set out the questions on which the ruling is sought, identifying the Treaty provisions or other Acts, Instruments or Rules of Community Law concerned).

Dated the　　　day of　　　19

Costs and Legal Aid

The Court of Justice established at an early stage that the costs of the parties incurred in respect of an Article 177 reference are incidental to the domestic proceedings. They are therefore reserved to and decided by the national court. The national court must reach a decision on costs in accordance with national law. Domestic legal aid may be available to assist the parties at the stage of the Article 177 reference. In civil proceedings the authority of the general committee is required before a legal aid certificate can extend to the proceedings in the Court of Justice. The Court of Justice itself has power to grant legal aid in special circumstances. An example would be where legal aid is not available in the national court.

References from the United Kingdom

There follows a list of cases referred to the European Court of Justice under Article 177 since 1 January 1988 from UK courts or tribunals. This list includes all cases awaiting judgment and those in which judgment was given during the period January to June 1990. The list, which is taken from a recent White Paper "Developments in the European Community" (January–June 1990 CM 1234), illustrates the wide range of circumstances in which points of Community law may come before the domestic courts and tribunals of the United Kingdom.

Cases referred to the European Court under Article 177 of the EEC Treaty from UK courts or tribunals

1. Case C-118/88 *Suffolk Coastal District Council* v *Notcutts Garden Centres Ltd* (compatibility of section 47 of Shops Act 1950 with Article 30 EEC Treaty). Removed from the Register.

2. Case C-126/88 *The Boots Company plc* v *Commissioners of Customs & Excise* (consideration of 6th VAT Directive purposes – special sales promotion). Judgment given 27 March 1990.

3. Case C-174/88 *R* v *Dairy Produce Quote Tribunal, ex parte Hall and Sons (Dairy Farmers) Ltd* (calculation of reference quantity of milk to be assigned to a producer). Judgment given 6 June 1990.

4. Case C-195/88 *Shrewsbury & Atcham Borough Council* v *B&Q plc* (compatibility of Section 47 of the Shops Act 1950 with Article 30 EEC Treaty).

5. Case C-232/88 *Derry City Council* v *Hampden Homecare plc* (compatibility of Section of the Shops Act (Northern Ireland) 1946 with Article 30 EEC Treaty).

6. Case C-262/88 *Barber* v *Guardian Royal Exchange* (application of Article 119 EEC Treaty and Equal Pay and Equal Treatment Directives to redundancy and pension payments to men and women at different ages). Judgment given 17 May 1990 [1990 2 CMLR 513.

7. Case C-291/88 *Torfaen Borough Council* v *Texas Homecare Ltd* (compatibility of Shops Act 1950 with Article 30 EEC Treaty). Removed from the Register 12 May 1990.

8. Case C-301/88 *R* v *IBAP, ex parte Fish Producers Organization and Grimsby Fish Producers Organization* (compensation for fish withdrawn failing to comply with marketing standards).

9. Case C-306/88 *Rochdale BC* v *Anders* (compatibility of Shops Act 1950 with Article 30 EEC Treaty).

10. Case C-331/88 *R* v *MAFF & Secretary of State for Health, ex parte FEDESA & others* (challenge to UK legislation implementing Hormones Directive).

11. Case C-333/88 *Peter John Krier Tither* v *Commissioners of the Inland Revenue* (exclusion from MIRAS of those specially exempt or immune from tax on salaries). Judgment given 22 March 1990.

12. Case C-370/88 *Procurator Fiscal, Stranraer* v *Andrew Marshall* (whether Articles 7 and 40(3) EEC prohibit carriage of certain type of net by fishing vessel. Validity of Article 19 of Regulation 171/83).

13. Case C-372/88 *Milk Marketing Board* v *Cricket St Thomas Estate* (interpretation of Article 25 of Regulation 804/68 as amended by Regu-

lation 1421/78 – whether exclusive purchasing right of MMB extends to pasteurised milk.) Judgment given 27 March 1990.

14. Case C-23/89 *Quietlynn Ltd* v *Southend BC* (compatibility of sex establishment licence requirements under Local Government (Misc Provisions) Act 1982 with Article 30 EEC Treaty).

15. Case C-71/89 *R* v *IBAP, ex parte BEOCO & Others* and Case C-72/89 *R* v *IBAP, ex parte Cargill* (validity of Regulation 1587/88 subsidy for rape seed).

16. Case C-188/89 *A Foster & Others* v *British Gas plc* (status of the corporation; sex discrimination in occupational retirement provisions).

17. Case C-213/89 *R* v *Secretary of State for Transport, ex parte Factortame Limited & others* (reference from House of Lords on availability of interim relief pending ECJ judgment). Judgment given 19 June 1990.

18. Case C-221/89 *R* v *Secretary of State for Transport, ex parte Factortame Limited & others* (reference from Divisional Court on compatibility of provisions of Merchant Shipping Act 1988 with the Common Fisheries Policy).

19. Case C-233/89 *Cray Precision Engineers Ltd* v *David William Clarke* (sex discrimination).

20. Case C-292/89 *R* v *Immigration Appeal Tribunal, ex parte Antonissen* (whether a Member State may require a national of another Member State to leave its territory if after six months from admission he has failed to enter employment: status of Council declaration on Minutes of a meeting adopting a Directive).

21. Case C-350/89 *Sheptonhurst Ltd* v *Newham London Borough Council* (licencing of sex shops and breach of Article 30).

22. Case C-355/89 *DHSS (Isle of Man)* v *Barr and Montrose Holdings Ltd* (undertaking employment in the Isle of Man without being an Isle

of Man worker and without a work permit – Article 4 of Protocol No 3 to the Act of Accession).

23. Case C-356/89 *Roger Stanton Newton* v *Chief Adjudication Officer* (whether mobility allowances falls within Article 4(1)(b) of Council Regulation 1408/71; application of Article 10 of the Regulation).

24. Case C-31/90 *Elsie Rita Johnson* v *Chief Adjudication Officer* (whether Directive 79/7 applies to persons who left employment for the purposes of child care and who were prevented from returning to employment due to illness).

25. Case C-38/90 *R* v *Thomas Edward Lomas* (the validity of Commission Regulation 1633/84 – clawback and sheepmeat).

26. Case C-84/90 *R* v *MAFF, ex parte John James Dent and Mary Astrid Dent* (Article 3A(2) of Council Regulation 857/84 adopting general rules for the application of the levy referred to in Regulation 804/68 (Article 5C) on reorganization of the market in milk and milk products).

27. Case C-151/90 *R* v *1. Robert Leslie Fletcher, 2. Jeremy Nicholas Pritchard, 3. North Riding Lamb Ltd* (validity of Article 4(1) and (2) of Regulation 1633/84 – rules for applying the variable slaughter premium of sheep).

28. Case C-191/90 *Generics (UK) Ltd. & another* v *Smith Kline & French Laboratories Ltd* (Articles 30 and 36 EEC Treaty. compatibility terms of licence: right to import patent products from outside EC provisions of Patents Act 1977.)

*Richard Whish, Professor of Law, King's College London; Partner and Head of EEC and Competition Law Department, Watson Farley and Williams

Chapter 3
The European Court of First Instance*

Introduction

1989 saw the birth of a new European Community court: the Court of
First Instance of the European Communities (the CFI). This is prob-
ably the biggest structural change to the Court of Justice of the European Communities (the ECJ) since it was transformed from the Court
of Justice of the European Coal and Steel Community to the Court of
Justice of the three European Communities in 1958. Its establishment
represents a major change in the administration of justice in the European Community

Origins of the Court of First Instance

There were essentially two reasons for establishing the CFI. The first
was to relieve the ECJ of part of its workload. Over the years the
number of cases brought before the ECJ had risen considerably[1] and
had risen more rapidly than the ECJ's capacity to dispose of cases. The
result was a significant build-up in the number of cases pending at the
end of a year[2] and a marked lenghthening of the time taken to deliver
judgments. Whereas a preliminary ruling took on average six months
in 1975, it took 18 months in 1988. Similarly, whereas direct actions
took on average nine months to come to judgment in 1975 they took 24
months in 1988. These delays became a subject of concern: in a direct
action with major financial interests at stake, a delay of two years could
cause the parties considerable hardship. With the prospect of an 18
month delay in obtaining a preliminary ruling there was also a danger
that national courts might be deterred from referring cases to the ECJ,

which could represent a risk for the uniformity of Community law. Therefore, one reason for setting up the CFI was to relieve the ECJ of part of its workload with a view to reducing these delays to more acceptable proportions.

The second main reason for establishing the CFI was to improve the administration of justice in the European Community. The ECJ had been criticised for its handling of cases requiring a close examination of complex facts, for example certain competition cases. Some commentators took the view that the ECJ did not always go into questions of fact adequately. The view was also expressed that, as a court of last resort, the ECJ was not the appropriate forum in which to resolve complex disputes on the facts. The second line of thought which led to the setting up the CFI was that it would be preferable to set up a first instance court specifically adapted to carrying out a close examination of complex facts.

These ideas took concrete form in the autumn of 1985. Quite late in the negotiations leading up to the adoption of the Single European Act, the ECJ suggested that provisions could be inserted in that Act providing for the establishment of a court of first instance. The suggestion was promptly taken up and it was agreed that the Single European Act would insert in the founding Treaties a provision empowering the Council to establish a court of first instance by a subsequent decision.

The Single European Act (OJ 1987 L169/1) was signed the following year, at Luxembourg on 17 February 1986 and at The Hague on 28 February 1986. After ratification it came into force on 1 July 1987. It inserted a new Article 168A into the EEC Treaty and identically worded provisions into the ECSC (a new Art 32D) and Euratom Treaties (a new Art 140A). For convenience reference will be made here only to the provisions of the EEC Treaty.

Article 168A of the EEC Treaty lays down the main features of the CFI. Article 168A(1) in particular provides:

"At the request of the Court of Justice and after consulting the Commission and the European Parliament, the Council may, acting unanimously, attach to the Court of Justice a court with jurisdiction to hear and determine at first instance, subject to a right of appeal to the Court of Justice on points of law only and in accordance with the conditions laid down by the Statute, certain classes of action or proceeding brought by natural or legal persons. That court shall not be competent to hear and determine actions brought by Member States or by Community institutions or questions referred for a preliminary ruling under Article 177".

Three salient points emerge from Article 168A(1). First, the jurisdiction of the CFI is extremely narrowly defined. It is confined to certain classes of action brought by natural or legal persons and excludes any action brought by a Member State or a Community Institution as well as any preliminary ruling. These limitations on the CFI's jurisdiction will continue to apply indefinitely and can only be relaxed by an amendment to the Treaties. Secondly, Article 168A(1) makes it clear that the decisions of the CFI at first instance are subject to a right of appeal to the ECJ "on points of law only". Thus, it is made clear in the Treaty that appeals are confined to points of law, although the exact meaning of that term is left to be defined subsequently. Finally, it emerges that the CFI is not to be a new institution in its own right but is to be "attached to" the ECJ.

Working within the framework of Article 168A of the EEC Treaty, the Council adopted a Decision establishing the CFI on 24 October 1988: Council Decision 88/591/ECSC, EEC, Euratom ("the Decision") (OJ 1988 L319/1; corrigendum OJ 1989 L241/4; corrected version OJ 1989 C215/1).

It took about a year to make the practical arrangements for the new court and to appoint its members. Then, pursuant to a decision of the President of the ECJ (OJ 1989 L317/48), it commenced operations on 31 October 1989.

One more important piece of legislation remains to be adopted, namely, the Rules of Procedure of the CFI. Under Article 168A(4) of the EEC Treaty the CFI is to establish its own Rules of Procedure in agreement with the ECJ and subject to the unanimous approval of the Council. (This has now been done – see Appendix.)

Composition and Organization of the Court of First Instance

The CFI consists of 12 members (Decision, Art 2(1)). They are chosen from persons whose independence is beyond doubt and who possess the ability required for appointment to judicial office. They are appointed by common accord of the Governments of the Member States (EEC

Treaty Art 168A(3)). Although in law there is no nationality requirement, the Member States appointed one member of the CFI from each Member State. The first members of the CFI are the following:

The Hon Mr Justice Donal Barrington (Ireland)
Born on 28 February 1928, Judge of the Irish High Court since 1979 and Member of the Special Criminal Court since 1987, previously Senior Counsel specialising in constitutional and commercial law.

Mr Jacques Biancarelli (France)
Born on 18 October 1948, Director of Legal Services at Crédit Lyonnais, former legal secretary at the ECJ.

Mr Cornelis Briët (Netherlands)
Born on 23 February 1944, Vice-President of the District Court of Rotterdam, Deputy Judge at the District Court of Middelburg and Deputy Judge at the Cantonal courts of Rotterdam, Brielle and Sommelsdijk.

Professor David Edward, CMG, QC (United Kingdom)
Born on 14 November 1934, Salvesen Professor of European Institutions at the University of Edinburgh, Honorary Sheriff at Perth and Chairman of Medical Appeal Tribunals.

Mr Rafael Garcia-Valdecasas y Fernandez (Spain)
Born in 1946, Spanish Government lawyer responsible for litigation before the ECJ and for negotiations on the establishment of the CFI.

Mr Heinrich Kirschner (Federal Republic of Germany)
Born on 7 January 1938, senior official in the Federal Ministry of Justice, earlier a judge in the Regional Court of Bochum and the Local Court of Wanne-Eickel.

Mr Koenraad Lenaerts (Belgium)
Born in 1954, Professor of Law at the Katholieke Universiteit Leuven, Visiting Professor at the University of Strasbourg and Professor at the College of Europe Bruges, former legal secretary at the ECJ.

Mr Antonio Saggio (Italy
Born in 1934, Judge of the Court of Cassation and Professor of Community law at the Scuola Superiore della Pubblica Amministrazione in Rome, former legal secretary at the ECJ.

Mr Romain Schintgen (Luxembourg)
Born on 22 March 1939, senior official in the Luxembourg Ministry of Labour, expert in labour law.

Mr Bo Vesterdorf (Denmark)
Born in 1945, senior official in the Danish Ministry of Justice, former lawyer-linguist at the ECJ.

Mr José Luis da Cruz Vilaça (Portugal)
Born on 20 September 1944, Professor of European Economy and International Economic Organizations at Lusiada University, former Advocate General at the ECJ.

Mr Christos Yeraris (Greece)
Born on 13 September 1938, Member of the Greek Council of State and lecturer in Community law at the National School of Public Administration and the Institute of Continuing Education.

The Portuguese Member, Mr Da Cruz Vilaça, was appointed President of the CFI.

The CFI does not have permanently appointed Advocates-General as does the ECJ, but it may call upon its members to perform the task of an Advocate-General in a particular case. The criteria for selecting such cases and the procedure for designating members of the CFI to act as Advocates-General have been laid down in the CFI's Rules of Procedure. For the time being members are called upon to act as Advocate-General on an *ad hoc* basis. Thus, the CFI has dealt with a number of staff cases without appointing an Advocate-General, but the German member, Mr Kirschner was appointed to act as Advocate-General in the competition case, *Tetra Pak* v *Commission*,[3] and the Danish member Mr Vesterdorf was appointed to act as Advocate-General in a series of competition cases known as the *Polypropylene* cases.[4]

The CFI normally sits in panels (called "Chambers") of three or five judges. It may also sit in plenary session. The composition of the Chambers and the assignment of cases to Chambers or to a plenary session are governed by the CFI's Rules of Procedure (Arts 10–16). For its initial period of operation the CFI had set up two five-judge Chambers and three three-judge Chambers, which may sit alternatively; and it has adopted the practice of assigning staff cases to the three-judge Chambers and others cases to the five-judge Chambers (OJ 1989 C281/2; OJ 1990 C199/9). Although it is envisaged that the CFI will normally sit in Chambers, its first hearing, in the *Tetra Pak* case on 14 December 1989, was held in plenary session.

The Members of the CFI each have their own personal staff of one legal assistant and one secretary. The CFI has its own Registrar (Mr Hans Jung, a former official of the ECJ) and its own Registry, but for the rest it shares the administrative "infrastructure" of the ECJ. Thus the two courts share the same interpretation service, the same translation department, the same library and so on. Physically, the CFI is housed in the same complex of buildings as the ECJ in Luxembourg, occupying an annex which has been christened "the Erasmus building".

Jurisdiction of the Court of First Instance

The jurisdication of the CFI is extremely narrow. Confined by Article 168A(1) of the EEC Treaty to actions brought by natural or legal persons, it was further restricted by the terms of Article 3 of the Decision to certain kinds of subject-matter. Article 3 transfers to the CFI the first instance jurisdiction of the ECJ in four specific categories of case:

(1) Staff cases, *i.e.* disputes between the Communities and their servants;

(2) Actions by undertakings against the Commission concerning the ECSC Treaty provisions on levies, production controls, price regulation or competition;

(3) Actions by natural or legal persons against a Community institution relating to the implementation of the EEC competition rules applicable to undertakings;

(4) Damages claims by natural or legal persons where the damage is alleged to arise from an act or failure to act which is the subject of an action, under 1, 2 or 3 above.

Staff cases are relatively numerous, accounting for nearly a fifth of the cases brought before the ECJ in recent years. However, although important to the staff involved, they are not directly concerned with the law on European integration and are seldom of interest to wider circles. The ECSC Treaty provided the ECJ with a steady flow of litigation throughout the 1980s as a result of the quota system imposed in the steel sector to manage the crisis which it was then going through. However, with the dismantlement of the quota system, that source of litigation has practically dried up. There remain the actions brought by natural or legal persons under the EEC competition rules applicable to undertakings. Category 4 above is not an independent category but only concerns damages claims linked to claims under one of the other three heads. Thus in effect, the jurisdiction of the CFI falls into two main categories: staff cases on the one hand and EEC competition cases brought by natural or legal persons on the other hand. At present the number of cases in each category is about equal.

It is of obvious interest to practitioners involved with competition cases to know that from now on a direct action in the competition field must be brought before the CFI and will only reach the ECJ if there is an appeal. The type of case involved will be an action by an undertaking contesting a Commission decision affecting it. Thus, a case such as Case 226/84 *British Leyland plc* v *Commission* [1986] ECR 3267, contesting a fine imposed by a Commission decision for an anti-competitive practice, is now within the jurisdiction of the CFI. A similar case now pending before the CFI is Case T-66/89 *Publishers' Association* v *Commission*, contesting the Commission's decision against the British Net Book Agreements. On the other hand, a competition case, even between undertakings, will still come before the ECJ if it originates before a national court and is sent for a preliminary ruling. There is perhaps a certain lack of symmetry in that distribution of jurisdiction, but it follows from the wording of Article 168A(1) of the EEC Treaty.

The Council, in adopting the Decision, transferred to the CFI only about three-quarters of the "classes of action or proceeding brought by natural or legal persons" which it could have transferred under Article

168A(1) of the EEC Treaty. One category in particular which was excluded from transfer, despite the fact that the ECJ proposed it, was cases concerning anti-dumping duties. The Council is, however, committed to re-examining the proposal to transfer anti-dumping cases after two years of operation of the CFI (Decision, Art 3(3)).

Other categories of case which were not transferred although they could have been include state aid cases brought by natural or legal persons, damages actions brought by natural or legal persons which are not connected to one of the defined heads of jurisdiction, cases brought by natural or legal persons under an arbitration clause in a contract with a Community Institution and certain miscellaneous annulment actions brought by natural or legal persons. All of these categories involve litigation of a kind well suited to a first instance court, frequently involving contested facts, and it might be appropriate for the Council to examine their transfer when it re-examines the transfer of anti-dumping cases to the CFI.

Procedure before the Court of First Instance

Procedure before the CFI is largely similar to that before the ECJ. This is particularly so during the period until the CFI adopted its own Rules of Procedure, because it had to use the ECJ's Rules of Procedure *mutatis mutandis* (Decision, Art 11). But even now, a basic similarity will still be ensured by the fact that the procedural provisions in the Statute of the ECJ have been made applicable almost in their entirety to the CFI, and the latter's Rules of Procedure are confined to laying down such further and more detailed provisions as may be necessary. (EEC, Art 168A(2) and EEC Statute, Art 46).

Hence the procedure before the CFI closely resembles that on a direct action before the ECJ. As before the ECJ, the written part of the procedure is substantially more important than the oral part of the procedure. The requirements for lodging a case before the CFI and the requirements regarding the written pleadings are substantially the same as before the ECJ. And the major stages of procedure are the same as those before the ECJ.

One major difference however concerns the Advocate-General. First, an Advocate-General is not necessarily appointed in every case and, secondly, the Advocate-General before the CFI may deliver his opinion in writing and does not have to read it out in open court as before the ECJ (EEC Statute, Art 46).

As regards the hearings of the parties, the CFI applies in principle the same restriction on the time allowed to the parties for their main speech (*i.e.* 15 minutes in a three-judge case and 30 minutes in a five-judge case, with questions and answers and replies to the other side coming on top of that basic allowance); but it appears that in practice the CFI is substantially more generous than the ECJ in granting extensions of that basic allowance at the request of the parties. Moreover, unlike the ECJ, if the CFI has granted more time to one party it automatically grants the same extensions to the other party. The willingness of the CFI to hold long hearings was strikingly illustrated by the recent hearing in the *Polypropylene* cases (see note 4 *supra*), which concerned an alleged cartel in the polypropylene industry and in which the facts were extensively disputed. The hearing lasted for six days, quite without parallel in the recent practice of the ECJ, which rarely allows the hearing in a case to exceed one day.

Finally, the CFI has in several cases held a preparatory meeting with the parties in advance of the hearing in cases where it judged that appropriate. These meetings may be in open court or *in camera*. Such a meeting might lead to the settlement of a case or clarify the issues and prepare the organization of a hearing in a case which is to go forward. The CFI's approach in such preparatory measures seems for the time being to be flexible and pragmatic.

Since it came into operation, the CFI has come to grips vigorously with its workload. At the time of writing it had held 78 hearings, of which 68 were in staff cases and 10 in competition cases. Within the same period the CFI had disposed of 78 cases, 58 by judgments and 20 orders terminating the proceedings (*e.g.* following a withdrawal or a finding or inadmissibility).

The hearings take place in new hearing rooms in the Erasmus building which are somewhat smaller than the hearing rooms of the ECJ. In the sittings the judges of the CFI wear dark blue robes, as compared with the maroon coloured robes of the members of the ECJ. The Erasmus building also houses the Registry of the CFI which is completely separate from that of the ECJ. Cases lodged before the CFI bear before their case number the prefix "T-" (*Tribunal de Première Instance*) whilst cases before the ECJ now bear the prefix "C-" (*Cour de Justice*). The judgments of the CFI will be published in the official *European Court Reports* (ECR) along with those of the ECJ.

Appeals to the European Court

The decisions of the CFI are subject to an appeal to the ECJ on points of law only (EEC, Art 168A(1) and EEC Statute, Art 51). At the time of writing 16 appeals had been lodged before the ECJ, 14 in staff cases and two in competition cases.

The procedure on appeal is based on that in a direct action before the ECJ but is more expeditious in a number of respects. Appeals may be brought within two months of the notification of the decision appealed against, and the opposing party has two months in which to lodge a response. Neither period can be extended. Basically there is only one round of written pleadings, and further pleadings may be lodged only with the express authorization of the President of the ECJ. Furthermore, the ECJ may dispense with the hearing of the parties unless one of the parties objects on the grounds that the written procedure did not enable him fully to defend his point of view (EEC statute, Act 52, and Rules of Procedure of the ECJ, Act 120(1)). In all cases, however, the Advocate-General before the ECJ delivers an opinion at a public sitting in the usual way.

Appeals lie on one of three grounds: lack of competence of the CFI, a breach of procedure before the CFI which adversely affects the interests of the appellant and infringement of Community law by the CFI. There is a parallel between these grounds and the grounds specified for an annulment action under Article 173 of the EEC Treaty. Where an appeal is, in whole or in part, clearly inadmissible or clearly unfounded, the ECJ may dismiss the appeal by reasoned order at any time, *e.g.* even before serving the appeal on the opposing party or before hearing argument from the parties (Rules of Procedure, Art 119). This power goes beyond the ECJ's powers to dismiss direct actions as inadmissible under Article 92 of its Rules of Procedure, because it allows the ECJ to dismiss appeals not only as inadmissible but also as unfounded. However, as a filter mechanism it does not go as far, for example, as the procedure of leave to appeal to the House of Lords in

England, which comprises a greater discretionary element.

If an appeal is well-founded the ECJ quashes the decision of the CFI. Thereupon, it may either give final judgment itself, where the state of the proceedings so permits, or refer the case back to the CFI for judgment (EEC Statute, Art 54). This is a pragmatic solution designed to ensure economy of procedure. Where a case is referred back to the CFI, that court will decide on costs; but where an appeal is dismissed or where an appeal is upheld and the case is settled by the ECJ itself, the ECJ makes the decision as to costs (Rules of Procedure of ECJ, Art 122).

Concluding remarks

If a large number of the decisions of the CFI are taken on appeal to the ECJ, the object of relieving the ECJ of part of its workload will not be achieved. Hence it is of interest to see, on the one hand, how restrictive will be the ECJ's treatment of the appeals brought before it in the common months, and on the other hand, how successfully the CFI establishes itself as a court whose decisions are sufficiently authoritative not to warrant an appeal. In that connection its vigorous business-like approach to its case load, and in particular its manner of preparing certain cases for the hearing, bode well for the future.

Pending the adoption of the CFI's own Rules of Procedure much interest has been focused on the provisions it will adopt in relation to fact-finding. However, at least as important is the practice which it develops in that regard. If it emerges as a successful fact-finding forum, it will have achieved the other object of its establishment which was to improve the quality of justice within the European Communities.

Finally, the question remains as to the extent of the CFI's jurisdiction. When the CFI started operations on 31 October 1989 it received only 151 cases by way of transfer from the 622 cases then pending before the ECJ. That left 471 cases still pending before the ECJ, which is substantially more than the ECJ has been able to dispose of in the average year recently. It thus seems that the transfer of jurisdiction to the CFI has been inadequate fully to relieve the ECJ of its workload. Reflections are already under way as to how the continuing backlog of the ECJ can be dealt with. Changes to the ECJ itself are one line of action; but as regards the CFI, increasing consideration is being given to an extension of its jurisdiction. First, some or all of the remaining categories of case covered by Article 168A of the EEC Treaty, in particular anti-dumping cases, may be transferred to the CFI. In the longer term, thought is being given to the possibility of further Treaty amendment to widen the jurisdiction of the CFI even beyond the limits currently imposed by Article 168A. If, as seems likely, the forthcoming arrangements for Economic and Monetary Union lead to the adoption of amendments to the Treaties, that could provide an opportunity for such amendment further extending the jurisdiction of the CFI. It has been remarkable to see the birth of a new Community court, and there is every possibility that the future will hold interesting new developments.

*Timothy Millett MA, Barrister. Principal Administrator at the Court of Justice of the European Communities. The views expressed are the author's own.
[1] From 79 in 1979 to around 400 a year in the late 1980s.
[2] *e.g.* 618 cases pending at the end of 1987 and 605 cases pending at the end of 1988.
[3] Case T-51/89, Opinion delivered on 21 February 1990, judgment delivered on 10 July 1990, not yet published.
[4] Joined Cases T-1–4 and 6–15/89, *Rhône-Poulenc and Others* v *Commission*, pending at the time of writing.

Chapter 4

How Limited is the Jurisdiction of the European Court of Justice?*

Introduction

The broad, purposive interpretation of substantive provisions of Community law by the European Court of Justice is so familiar as virtually to be regarded as the trademark of the European Court. Such an approach has also been followed with regard to the Treaty provisions concerning the jurisdiction of the European Court. Indeed, by now, we have even become used to the idea that the remedies expressed in one Treaty, may be extended to, or applied by analogy to, situations governed by another Treaty. So, for example, in Case 9/56 *Meroni* [1957 and 1950] ECR 133, the narrow version of the plea of illegality contained in Article 36 of the ECSC Treaty, under which the illegality of an underlying general decision may be invoked only where the applicant is seeking the annulment of a decision imposing a pecuniary sanction or period penalty payment, was held to be a specific application of the more general principle recognised in the EEC and Euratom Treaties allowing the applicant to question the legality of the general legislation on which any individual decision is based. Similarly, as recently as last year, the Court held that although Article 41 of the ECSC Treaty gave it power only to consider the validity of Community legislation on a reference from a national court, nonetheless it would be inconsistent with the logic of the Treaties for it to have power to interpret Community law under the corresponding provision of the EEC and Euratom Treaties, but have no power to do so in the context of the ECSC Treaty (Case C-221/88 *ECSC* v *Busseni* – judgment of 22 February 1990). The European Court therefore arrogated to itself also jurisdiction to interpret provisions of legislation made under the ECSC Treaty on a reference from a national court. In the meantime, in the first of the cases to be brought by Luxembourg against the European Parliament in an attempt to challenge the Parliament's decisions as to where it should sit (Case 230/81 *Luxembourg* v *European Parliament* [1983] ECR 255), the Court allowed Article 38 of the ECSC Treaty, which alone among the Treaties expressly envisages an action for annulment being brought against the European Parliament, to be used to challenge a resolution of the Parliament which produced effects, indeed most of its effects, under the other Treaties. However, the purpose of this paper is not so much to examine those situations where a lawyer trained in the common law tradition might say that the European Court has stretched an express jurisdiction, but rather to investigate whether the European Court is beginning to assert a general jurisdiction, that is, a jurisdiction which does not rest on the express terms of those provisions of the Treaty which deal with the Court's jurisdiction, and also to investigate whether it is beginning to adopt practices which cannot in themselves be said to be derived from Treaties.

Acts susceptible to annulment

A common factor in the actions for annulment envisaged in all three Community Treaties is that non-binding acts, such as opinions, may not be challenged. Nevertheless, such non-binding acts may still have important legal effects, and at a very early stage, in the mid-1950s, the European Court can be found developing a technique to enable judicial control to be exercised in such cases. The point first seems to have arisen in Cases 1 & 15/57 *Usines à Tubes de la Sarre* [1957 and 1958] ECR 105. This case involved an opinion under Article 54 of the ECSC Treaty on an investment proposal submitted by the applicant. Under the terms of the ECSC Treaty, such opinions must be reasoned. The Court, however, found as a fact that there was no statement of reasons accompanying the opinion, and formally held that in the absence of a statement of reason the opinion could not exist. Whatever the conceptual niceties involved in distinguishing an act which does not exist from one which is a nullity, a declaration of inexistence is in practical terms very similar to a declaration of nullity. In particular, it means that any procedure in which a reasoned opinion is required will inevitably be defective if there is held to be no reasoned opinion.

While, as has been mentioned above, the ECSC Treaty does contain a remedy enabling acts of the European Parliament to be challenged, there is no such provision in the EEC and Euratom Treaties. In 1986, the European Court went beyond holding that the Coal and Steel remedy could be used against acts which also produced effects under the EEC and Euratom Treaties to allow an action to be brought under Article 173 of the EEC Treaty against an act of the European Parliament. The point arose in Case 294/83 *"Les Verts"* v *European Parliament* [1986] ECR 1339 which involved a challenge by the French Greens to decisions of, and rules adopted by, the European Parliament concerning appropriations granted as a contribution to the information campaign for the second direct elections to the Parliament. Despite the silence of Article 173 of the EEC Treaty, which refers only to acts of the Council and the Commission, the Court held that the general scheme of the Treaty was to make a direct action available against all measures adopted by the institutions which are intended to have legal effects. The Court suggested that the European Parliament was not expressly mentioned amongst the institutions whose measures might be contested because in its original version the EEC Treaty merely granted it powers of consultation and political control, rather than the power to adopt measures intended to have legal effects vis-à-vis third parties. Since, unlike the ECSC Treaty, the EEC Treaty contained only one provision relating to an action for annulment, Article 173, the Court held that this provision must be regarded as being of general application. It further held that an interpretation of it which excluded measures adopted by the European Parliament from those which could be contested would lead to a result contrary both to the spirit of the Treaty and to its system. If Article 173 were not so extended, measures adopted by the European Parliament in the context of the EEC Treaty could trespass into the powers of the Member States or of the other institutions or exceed the limits set for the Parliament's powers, without it being possible to refer them for review by the Court. Whilst this approach does not perhaps take into account the Court's early case law holding that Acts which cannot be annuled may nonetheless be regarded as non-existent, the Court went on to conclude that an action for annulment must lie against measures adopted by the European

Parliament intended to have legal effects with regard to third parties. With regard to the particular decisions and rules of the European Parliament at issue, the Court held that they governed the rights and obligations both of those political groupings that were already represented in the European Parliament, and of those which wished to take part in the 1984 direct elections. The measures were therefore designed to produce legal effects with regard to third parties and could be the subject of an action for annulment under Article 173. In other words, so as to ensure a comprehensive system of judicial control of acts of the Community institutions affected the legal situation of third parties, the European Court re-wrote Article 173 so as to include the European Parliament as the author of a challengeable act.

Actions by the European Parliament

In "*Les Verts*", the European Parliament did not dispute that in areas where it may itself adopt legal measures, it was subject to judicial review by the Court. However, it would appear that this concession was made so as to enable it to argue that it should in turn have the capacity to bring an action for annulment against measures adopted by the Council and the Commission. In so claiming, the Parliament was moving into an area where none of the Treaties give it *locus standi*. While the action for failure to act under Article 175 of the EEC Treaty did not in fact give rise to much difficulty, since it expressly allows an action to be brought by any of the institutions, Article 173 of the EEC Treaty restricts the direct action for annulment to the Council and the Commission of the Community institutions, and Articles 33 and 38 of the ECSC Treaty are similarly limited. The Parliament did, however, attempt to bring direct action for annulment in Case 302/87 *European Parliament* v *Council* [1988] ECR 5615. It there sought to challenge the Council decision laying down general rules, pursuant to the Single European Act, for delegating powers to the Commission, otherwise rejoicing in the name of comitology. The Court there suggested that there was no necessary correlation between the ability to be the defendant in an action for annulment and the ability to bring such an action. It further indicated that the remedies available to the European Parliament were essentially political, in particular censure of the Commission, and that if the European Parliament wished action to be taken before the Court against another institution it should in principle ask the Commission to act on its behalf.

However, the European Court has now been persuaded to change its mind in Case C-70/88 *European Parliament* v *Council* (decision of 22 May 1990) with regard to legislation laying down maximum levels of radio-active contamination for foodstuffs following a nuclear accident. Although this action was brought against the Council of Ministers, in reality the Parliament was challenging the action of the Commission, which had put forward the proposal for this legislation on the legal basis of Article 31 of the Euratom Treaty, which merely required the Parliament to be consulted, whereas the Parliament argued that it should have been based on Article 100A of the EEC Treaty, which would have required the use of the co-operation procedure with Parliament. The Parliament therefore argued that the second case showed that the Commission could not be relied upon to act on its behalf to challenge a measure where the Commission itself had drafted that meaasure on a legal basis other than that considered appropriate by Parliament. The Parliament therefore suggested that there was a lacuna which the Court should fill by allowing the European Parliament to bring an action for annulment at least insofar as that was necessary to protect its own prerogatives. Interestingly, the Commission, whilst intervening to support the Council on the substance, nevertheless supported the Parliament's arguments with regard to admissibility.

After having noted that the Parliament was not expressly mentioned either in Article 173 of the EEC Treaty or Article 146 of the Euratom Treaty, the Court also pointed out that the Parliament could not bring an action as a legal person under the second paragraph of those provisions, because it did not itself enjoy legal personality. After having referred to the 1988 judgment, the Court accepted that the second case did indeed show that there may be circumstances where the remedies available to the European Parliament were either ineffective or uncertain, in particular noting that although the Commission may in principle be obliged to ensure that the prerogatives of the Parliament are respected, this could not go to the extent of requiring the Commission to bring an action for annulment which it itself believed to be ill conceived. The Court therefore concluded that the remedies available under the Treaties were not adequate to ensure the proper control of an act of the Council or Commission which breached the prerogatives of the Parliament. The Court further suggested that the institutional balance established by the Treaties required each of the institutions to exercise its powers in such a manner as to respect the powers of the other institutions, which in particular implied that a breach of that principle should be subject to judicial control. The Court therefore held that a judicial remedy must be available to ensure respect for the Parliament's prerogatives.

However, the Court was not willing simply to add the Parliament to the Council and Commission as privileged litigants under Article 173 of the EEC or Article 146 of the Euratom Treaty; rather, it suggested that Parliament would be required to show that it had an interest in bringing the action. Nonetheless, the Parliament's prerogatives could not be breached without a judicial remedy being available and the failure to make such a provision in the Treaties must give way to the fundamental interest in maintaining respect for the institutional balance established by the Treaties. The Court, therefore, in effect created a new version of the action for annulment for the Parliament; it held that the Parliament could bring an action for annulment before the Court directed against an action of the Council or the Commission on condition that this action was intended to safeguard the Parliament's prerogatives, and that it was based on the grounds relating to the violation of those prerogatives. Amongst those prerogatives was the Parliament's role in the legislative process, in particular its right to participate in the co-operation procedure. Therefore, in claiming that a Treaty base had been used which deprived it of the opportunity to participate in the co-operation procedure, the Parliament was indeed invoking an alleged breach of its prerogatives. It may, however, be suggested that this new remedy is not totally without parallels. During the course of the 1980s, when faced with the well known problems of direct and individual concern, and the substantive problem of knowing whether a refusal to act on the part of the Community institution itself amounts to a challengeable act or a failure to act, the Court developed the theory that where a particular procedure was laid down by Community law, a litigant who had participated in that procedure could bring an action for annulment to ensure that that procedure had been correctly followed with regard to that particular participant. This approach was first laid down in Case 191/82 *Fedrol* v *Commission* [1983] ECR 2913 with regard to dumping complaints, in which area it was reaffirmed in the *Timex* case (Case 264/82 [1985] ECR 849), and it has subsequently been extended for example to the area of complaints about state aids, in the *Cofaz* case (Case 169/84 [1986] ECR 391). It might be suggested that the 1990 *Parliament* v *Council* judgment falls into this line, in that where a procedure is laid down for the Parliament's participation, the action for annulment is available to the European Parliament to ensure that that procedure is followed. Nevertheless, the remedy is indeed one which does not self-evidently flow from the terms of the Treaty.

Precedent

One interesting sidelight of the 1990 *Parliament* v *Council* case, is the approach taken by the Court to distinguishing its previous decisions. We are by now familiar with the Court quoting its previous decisions when it is following them; indeed, citation of a previous judgment appears frequently to be regarded as a sufficient reason not to have to give a detailed reasoning of the same point again in the Court's judgments. On the other hand, it has long been notorious that the European Court does not state directly when it is not following its earlier case law. What was novel about the judgment in the Parliament's case was that the Court referred expressly to its 1988 judgment, referred in detail to the reasoning in that judgment, and then concluded that the remedies it had suggested that the Parliament should use in that judgment were not in fact sufficiently effective or certain. The Court then went on openly to reach a different conclusion. This approach has been repeated in a different area Case C-10/89 *CNL-SUCAL* v *HAG* (17 October 1990). This case involved once again the famous HAG trademark which had been at issue in Case 192/73 *van Zuylen* v *HAG* [1974] ECR 731. It will be remembered that in that case the European Court laid down the doctrine of common origin, stating that the holder of a trademark having the same origin as that used by a trader in another Member State could not invoke it to prevent imports under that mark from the Member State. That doctrine had been heavily criticised, and in the 1990 judgment, the European Court expressly stated in as many words that it found it necessary to reconsider the interpretation given in the earlier judgment in the light of its later case law. After expressly reaffirming the approach derived from the *Centrafarm* cases (Cases 15 & 16/74 [1974] ECR 1147 and 1183) that where a product has been sold by the holder of the patent or trademark himself or with his consent in one Member State, then the owner of the right cannot prevent those goods being imported into another Member State where he holds the rights, the Court expressly reversed the common origin rule, at least where the right to the mark had at some stage been expropriated so that the marks were operated independently. Could it be suggested that these decisions indicate a subtle change in the Court's attitude to precedent; no longer are earlier cases merely something which save detailed reasoning in later cases, but they are of sufficient importance as sources of law for the Court to need to state expressly when it is no longer following them. In effect, the attitude of the Court to its previous decisions appears to be taking a distinctly English turn.

Towards a general jurisdiction?

Whilst the Parliament cases mentioned above see the Court extending a well-established remedy, or at least a version of a well-established remedy, to situations that were not expressly provided for in the Treaty, another recent decision of the Court involves a remedy which was not foreseen by those who drafted the Treaties, and involves a jurisdiction asserted upon the basis of general provisions of the Treaty. This was Case C-2/88 *IMM Zwartveld* (13 July 1990), which involved a request by a Dutch court for the European Court to give it assistance in a case before it. The Dutch judge was investigating an alleged fraud involving breaches of the Community fish quota system, and the fish marketing system. The Dutch judge claimed that in order to proceed with his investigation he needed access to certain reports prepared by Commission officials, and also required those officials to give evidence before him. The Commission refused to transmit the reports to the Dutch judge, so he then sent a request to the European Court asking it to order the Commission to produce the documents and to order the inspectors to give evidence before him. The Dutch judge was obviously aware of the difficulty of finding a legal base on which the European Court could act, but he himself invoked Articles 1 and 12 of the Protocol on the Privileges and Immunities of the European Communities; Article 1 provides that the property and assets of the Communities shall not be subject to legal measures of constraint without the authorization of the Court of Justice, and Article 12 provides, amongst other things, that the immunity of Community officials with regard to acts performed by them in their official capacity is subject to the jurisdiction of the Court in disputes between the Communities and their officials and other servants. He also invoked the Council of Europe conventions on assistance in criminal matters, on the basis that, although the Community itself was not a party to them, nonetheless they should be considered as forming an integral part of the Community legal order, which itself indicates an interesting development of the Court's well-known case law holding that the principles underlying the European Convention on Human Rights are general principles which must be recognized within the Community context, even though the Community itself is not a party to the Human Rights convention. (See for example Case 36/75 *Rutili* [1975] ECR 1219 and 1232.)

The reaction of the Commission was to argue that the Dutch judge's application was inadmissible. It argued that the Treaty must be regarded as exhaustive with regard to the remedies available before the European Court, and it emphasised that the only way a national court could bring a matter before the European Court was by reference under Article 177 of the EEC Treaty, and in the Commission's view that was not relevant because the Dutch judge was not seeking the interpretation of a provision of Community law. The Commission also suggested that Articles 1 and 12 of the Protocol on the Privileges and Immunities of the European Communities were not relevant in this context. Asked by the Court as to its substantive reasons for refusing to produce the reports or to allow its inspectors to give evidence, the Commission took the line that its inspectors' reports were internal documents which did not necessarily reflect the Commission's position, and their communication could harm relations between the Commission and Member States in the delicate area of supervision of the fisheries market. The Commission also invoked Article 2 of the Protocol on Privileges and Immunities, which provides that the archives of the Communities shall be inviolable; the Commission claimed that Article 2 contained no exemptions, so that the Court had no power to lift that immunity.

With regard to the appearance of its inspectors as witnesses, the Commission indicated that it was not willing to indicate the identity of its inspectors or to authorise them to give evidence, because if they did so, it would affect their work and the degree to which they were able to exercise effective supervision on behalf of the Community. On the other hand, the Commission did declare its willingness to prepare a report for the Dutch judge to the extent that this would not compromise the Commission's supervisory functions, and that it might designate specific officials to give evidence before the Dutch judge, but he in turn refused to accept this offer.

Following a procedure analogous to that which would have been used if this had been a reference for a preliminary ruling under Article 177 of the EEC Treaty, the Court invited the Community institutions and the Member States to submit observations, and such observations received from the Council, the Parliament, Germany, France, Greece, Ireland, Italy, the Netherlands, Portugal, and the United Kingdom. Obviously, the case aroused a great deal of interest.

The Court's own reasoning began with a reference back to the famous case of *Costa* v *ENEL* (Case 6/64 [1964] ECR 585), emphasising the passage in that judgment which held that the EEC Treaty had created its own legal system which became an integral part of the legal systems of the Member States. The Court then referred to its judgment in the *"les Verts"* case, which has been discussed above, pointing out that the EC is a Community based on law, to the extent that neither the Member States nor the institutions may escape from judicial control over the conformity of their actions to the Treaty, which the Court described as a constitutional charter. It went on to say that in this Community based on law the relationship between the Member States and the Community institutions is governed, by virtue of Article 5 of the Treaty, by the principle of loyal co-operation, which not only requires that Member States take all necessary measures to guarantee the effective implementation of Community law, including the use of criminal penalties if necessary, but this principle also required the Community institutions to observe reciprocal duties of loyal co-operation with the Member States. This duty to co-operate was of particular importance in the relationship with national judicial autho-rities responsible for ensuring respect for Community law within the national legal order. In the light of this, the Court held that the privileges and immunities of the Communities were not absolute, and that the specific privileges and immunities accorded to Community officials were for their own personal protection. The Protocol could not therefore be used to avoid the duty of loyal co-operation owed to national judicial authorities. The Court suggested that where a request for information or evidence came from a national judge who was investigating alleged breaches of Community law, it was the duty of any Community institution, and in particular of the Commission en-trusted with ensuring that the provisions of the Treaty are applied, to give active support to the national judge by handing over the docu-ments and authorising the officials to give evidence.

In seeking to establish its own authority to order the Commission to comply with this basic duty of loyal co-operation, the Court invoked Article 164 of the Treaty, under which the Court is required to ensure that in the interpretation and application of the Treaty the law is observed. The Court held that by virtue of this provision it must ensure that an appropriate remedy must be available to enable it to exercise judicial control over the Commission's performance of its duty of loyal co-operation towards a national judicial authority. The Court there-fore held it had jurisdiction to examine in this particular instance whether the refusal to co-operate was justified in the light of a need to avoid interference with the operation and independence of the Com-munities. The Commission was therefore ordered to deliver the docu-ments requested by the Dutch judge to him, and to authorise its officials to give evidence before him, unless it could show that there were imperative reasons relating to the operation or independence of the Communities which would justify the refusal to deliver those docu-ments or to authorise that evidence to be given.

In fact, therefore, the Court would appear to have granted a new remedy not expressly foreseen in the Treaties, by virtue of two general provisions of the Treaty, Articles 5 and 164. Reference to Article 164 as a basis for the Court's action is not however totally new; in Case 17/74 *Transocean Marine Paint Association* v *Commission* [1974] ECR 1063, Advocate-General Warner suggested that Article 164 was a legal basis under which the European Court could take account of general principles of law derived from the laws of the Member States, on the basis that they formed part of "the law", of which it was the Court's duty to ensure the observance. The use of Articles 5 and 164 in combination, however, seems somewhat redolent of the technique used by the Commission to give itself legislative power on the basis of Article 5 and Article 155. This technique has been used by the Commission in the agricultural sector to fill the void when the Council has failed to exercise its legislative powers by the time it should have done, and came particularly to light in the context of the cereals market in 1985. There, faced with the Council's failure to adopt a Regulation on cereals prices based on a Commission proposal which would have led to price reductions even in nominal terms, and where therefore it would have been undesirable to allow the previous year's higher prices to be continued, the Commission enacted its own decision, and subsequently its own Regulation (Reg 2124/85, OJ 1985 L198/31) applying what it called "precautionary measures" (in other words, fixing lower prices) in the cereals market. In so doing the Commission claimed to act on the basis of Articles 5 and 155 of the Treaty, presumably invoking Article 5 on the basis that the failure of Member States meeting in Council to fix the cereal prices in due time constituted a breach of their duties under Article 5 to take all appropriate measures to ensure fulfilment of the obligations resulting from the action taken by the institutions of the Community, and invoking Article 155, which empowers the Commission to ensure that the provisions of the Treaty and the measures taken by the institutions pursuant thereto are applied, on the basis that in order to ensure the application of the common organization of marketing cereals it was necessary to fix prices. It is worth noting that no direct challenge was mounted to the Commission's action, and that the Commission has repeated the same technique on a number of subsequent occasions, most recently in Regulation 3890/90 (OJ 1990 L367/154) on temporary measures in the sheep meat sector.

It may be suggested that the reason the Commission's action was not challenged, whatever may be thought of its legal basis, is that in practical terms it was useful. Similarly, it might be suggested that it would be a serious lacuna in the Community legal system if no court had power to order a Community institution to co-operate with a national judicial authority seeking to enforce rules of Community law.

However, the door would appear to have been opened to the exercise of new sorts of judicial control in the complex relationship between Community institutions and Member States, going beyond the broad interpretation which the Court had already given to the express powers under the Treaties.

*Professor John A Usher, Professor of European Law, University of Exeter.

Appendix

Rules of Procedure of the Court of First Instance of the European Communities*

THE COURT OF FIRST INSTANCE OF THE EUROPEAN
COMMUNITIES,

Having regard to Article 32D of the Treaty establishing the European Coal
and Steel Community,

Having regard to Article 168A of the Treaty establishing the European
Economic Community,

Having regard to Article 140A of the Treaty establishing the European
Atomic Energy Community,

Having regard to the Protocol on the Statute of the Court of Justice of the
European Coal and Steel Community, signed in Paris on 18 April 1951,

Having regard to the Protocol on the Statute of the Court of Justice of the
European Economic Community, signed in Brussels on 17 April 1957,

Having regard to the Protocol on the Statute of the Court of Justice of the
European Atomic Energy Community, signed in Brussels on 17 April 1957,

Having regard to Council Decision 88/591/ECSC, EEC, Euratom of 24 Octo-
ber 1988 establishing a Court of First Instance of the European Communities
(OJ 1988 L319, with corrigendum in OJ 1989 L241), and in particular
Article 11 thereof,

Having regard to the agreement of the Court of Justice,

Having regard to the unanimous approval of the Council, given on 21 December 1990 and 29 April 1991,

Whereas the Court of First Instance is to establish its rules of procedure in agreement with the Court of Justice and with the unanimous approval of the Council and to adopt them immediately upon its consitution;

Whereas it is necessary to adopt the provisions laid down for the functioning of the Court of First Instance by the Treaties, by the Protocols on the Statutes of the Court of Justice and by the Council Decision of 24 October 1988 establishing a Court of First Instance of the European Communities and to adopt any other provisions necessary for applying and, when required, supplementing those instruments;

Whereas it is necessary to lay down for the Court of First Instance procedures adapted to the duties of such a court and to the task entrusted to the Court of First Instance of ensuring effective judicial protection of individual interests in cases requiring close examination of complex facts;

Whereas it is, moreover, desirable that the rules applicable to the procedure before the Court of First Instance should not differ more than is necessary from the rules applicable to the procedure before the Court of Justice under its Rules of Procedure adopted on 4 December 1974 (OJ 1974 L 350), as subsequently amended,

adopts the following

Rules of Procedure

Interpretation

Article 1

In these Rules:

"ECSC Treaty"	means the Treaty establishing the European Coal and Steel Community;
"ECSC Statute"	means the Protocol on the Statute of the Court of Justice of the European Coal and Steel Community;
"EEC Treaty"	means the treaty establishing the European Community;
"EEC Statute"	means the Protocol on the Statute of the Court of Justice of the European Economic Community;
"Euratom Treaty"	means the Treaty establishing the European Atomic Energy Community (Euratom);
"Euratom Statute"	means the Protocol on the Statute of the Court of Justice of the European Atomic Energy Community.

For the purposes of these Rules "institutions" means the institutions of the European Communities and the European Investment Bank.

Title 1 **Organization of the Court of First Instance**

Chapter 1

President and members of the Court of First Instance

Article 2

1) Every Member of the Court of First Instance shall, as a rule, perform the function of Judge.

   Members of the Court of First Instance are hereinafter referred to as "Judges".

2) Every Judge, with the exception of the President, may, in the circumstances specified in Articles 17 to 19, perform the function of Advocate-General in a particular case.

   References to the Advocate-General in these Rules shall apply only where a Judge has been designated as Advocate-General.

Article 3

The term of office of a Judge shall begin on the date laid down in his instrument of appointment. In the absence of any provision regarding the date, the term shall begin on the date of the instrument.

Article 4

1) Before taking up his duties, a Judge shall take the following oath before the Court of Justice of the European Communities: "I swear that I will perform my duties impartially and conscientiously; I swear that I will preserve the secrecy of the deliberations of the Court."

2) Immediately after taking the oath, a Judge shall sign a declaration by which he solemnly undertakes that, both during and after his term of office, he will respect the obligations arising therefrom, and in particular the duty to behave with integrity and discretion as regards the acceptance, after he has ceased to hold office, of certain appointments and benefits.

Article 5

When the Court of Justice is called upon to decide, after consulting the Court of First Instance, whether a Judge of the Court of First Instance no longer fulfils the requisite conditions or no longer meets the obligations arising from his office, the President of the Court of First Instance shall invite the Judge concerned to make representations to the Court of First Instance, in closed session and in the absence of the Registrar.

The Court of First Instance shall state the reasons for its opinion.

An opinion to the effect that a Judge of the Court of First Instance no longer fulfills the requisite conditions or no longer meets the obligations arising from his office must receive the votes of at least seven Judges of the Court of First Instance. In that event, particulars of the voting shall be communicated to the Court of Justice.

Voting shall be by secret ballot; the Judge concerned shall not take part in the deliberations.

Article 6

With the exception of the President of the Court of First Instance and of the Presidents of the Chambers, the Judges shall rank equally in precedence according to their seniority in office.

Where there is equal seniority in office, precedence shall be determined by age. Retiring Judges who are reappointed shall retain their former precedence.

Article 7

1) The Judges shall immediately after the partial replacement provided for in Article 32 (d) of the ECSC Treaty, Article 168(a) of the EEC Treaty and Article 140(a) of the Euratom Treaty, elect one of their number as President of the Court of First Instance for a term of three years.

2) If the office of the President of the Court of First Instance falls vacant before the normal date of expiry thereof, the Court of First Instance shall elect a successor for the remainder of the term.

3) The elections provided for in this article shall be by secret ballot. If a Judge obtains an absolute majority he shall be elected. If no Judge obtains an absolute majority, a second ballot shall be held and the Judge obtaining the most votes shall be elected. Where two or more Judges obtain an equal number of votes the oldest of them shall be deemed elected.

Article 8

The President of the Court of First Instance shall direct the judicial business and the administration of the Court of First Instance. He shall preside at plenary sittings and deliberations.

Article 9

When the President of the Court of First Instance is absent or prevented from attending or when the office of President is vacant, the functions of President shall be exercised by a President of a Chamber according to the order of precedence laid down in Article 6.

If the President of the Court and the Presidents of the Chambers are all prevented from attending at the same time, or their posts are vacant at the same time, the functions of President shall be exercised by one of the other Judges according to the order of precedence laid down in Article 6.

Chapter 2

Constitution of the Chambers and designation of Judge-Rapporteurs and Advocates-General

Article 10

1) The Court of First Instance shall set up Chambers composed of three or five Judges and shall decide which Judges shall be attached to them.
2) The composition of the Chambers shall be published in the *Official Journal of the European Communities*.

Article 11

1) Cases before the Court of First Instance shall be heard by Chambers composed in accordance with Article 10.

    Cases may be heard by the Court of First Instance sitting in plenary session under the conditions laid down in Articles 14, 51, 106, 118, 124, 127 and 129.
2) In cases coming before a Chamber, the term "Court of First Instance" in these Rules shall designate that Chamber.

Article 12

1) Subject to the provisions of Article 14, disputes between the Communities and their servants shall be assigned to Chambers of three Judges.

    Other cases shall, subject to the provisions of Article 14, be assigned to Chambers of five Judges.
2) The Court of First Instance shall lay down criteria by which, as a rule, cases are to be assigned to Chambers composed of the same number of Judges.

Article 13

1) As soon as the application initiating proceedings has been lodged, the President of the Court of First Instance shall assign the case to one of the Chambers.
2) The President of the Chamber shall propose to the President of the Court of

First Instance, in respect of each case assigned to the Chamber, the designation of a Judge to act as Rapporteur; the President of the Court of First Instance shall decide on the proposal.

Article 14

Whenever the legal difficulty or the importance of the case or special circumstances so justify, a case may be referred to the Court of First Instance sitting in plenary session or to a Chamber composed of a different number of Judges. Any decision to refer a case shall be taken under the conditions laid down in Article 51.

Article 15

The Court of First Instance shall appoint for a period of one year the Presidents of the Chambers.

The provisions of Article 7 (2) and (3) shall apply.

The appointments made in pursuance of this article shall be published in the *Official Journal of the European Communities*.

Article 16

In cases coming before a Chamber the powers of the President shall be exercised by the President of the Chamber.

Article 17

When the Court of First Instance sits in plenary session, it shall be assisted by an Advocate-General designated by the President of the Court of First Instance.

Article 18

A Chamber of the Court of First Instance may be assisted by an Advocate-General if it is considered that the legal difficulty or the factual complexity of the case so requires.

Article 19

The decision to designate an Advocate-General in a particular case shall be taken by the Court of First Instance sitting in plenary session at the request of the Chamber before which the case comes.

The President of the Court of First Instance shall designate the Judge called upon the perform the function of Advocate-General in that case.

Chapter 3

Registry

Section 1 – The Registrar

Article 20

1) The Court of First Instance shall appoint the Registrar.
   Two weeks before the date fixed for making the appointment, the President of the Court of First Instance shall inform the Judges of the applications which have been submitted for the post.
2) An application shall be accompanied by full details of the candidate's age, nationality, university degrees, knowledge of any languages, present and past occupations and experience, if any, in judicial and international fields.
3) The appointment shall be made following the procedure laid down in Article 7 (3).
4) The Registrar shall be appointed for a term of six years. He may be re-appointed.
5) Before he takes up his duties the Registrar shall take the oath before the Court of First Instance in accordance with Article 4.
6) The Registrar may be deprived of his office only if he no longer fulfils the requisite conditions or no longer meets the obligations arising from his office; the Court of First Instance shall take its decision after giving the Registrar an opportunity to make representations.
7) If the office of Registrar falls vacant before the usual date of expiry of the term thereof, the Court of First Instance shall appoint a new Registrar for a term of six years.

Article 21

The Court of First Instance may, following the procedure laid down in respect of the Registrar, appoint one or more Assistant Registrars to assist the Registrar and to take his place in so far as the Instructions to the Registrar referred in Article 23 allow.

Article 22

Where the Registrar is absent or prevented from attending and, if necessary, where the Assistant Registrar is absent or so prevented, or where the posts are vacant, the President of the Court of First Instance shall designate an official or servant to carry out the duties of Registrar.

Article 23

Instructions to the Registrar shall be adopted by the Court of First Instance acting on a proposal from the President of the Court of First Instance.

Article 24

1) There shall be kept in the Registry, under the control of the Registrar, a register initialled by the President of the Court of First Instance, in which all pleadings and supporting documents shall be entered in the order in which they are lodged.

2) When a document has been registered, the Registrar shall make a note to that effect on the original and, if a party so requests, on any copy submitted for the purpose.

3) Entries in the register and the notes provided for in the preceding paragraph shall be authentic.

4) Rules for keeping the register shall be prescribed by the Instructions to the Registrar referred to in Article 23.

5) Persons having an interest may consult the register at the Registry and may obtain copies or extracts on payment of a charge on a scale fixed by the Court of First Instance on a proposal from the Registrar.
   The parties to a case may on payment of the appropriate charge also obtain copies of pleadings and authenticated copies of orders and judgments.

6) Notice shall be given in the *Official Journal of the European Communities* of the date of registration of an application initiating proceedings, the names and addresses of the parties, the subject-matter of the proceedings, the form of order sought by the applicant and a summary of the pleas in law and of the main supporting arguments.

7) Where the Council or the Commission is not a party to a case, the Court of First Instance shall send to it copies of the application and of the defence, without the annexes thereto, to enable it to assess whether the inapplicability of one of its acts is being invoked under the third paragraph of Article 36 of the ECSC Treaty, Article 184 of the EEC Treaty or Article 156 of the Euratom Treaty.

Article 25

1) The Registrar shall be responsible, under the authority of the President, for the acceptance, transmission and custody of documents and for effecting service as provided for by these Rules.

2) The Registrar shall assist the Court of First Instance, the Chambers, the President and the Judges in all their official functions.

Article 26

The Registrar shall have custody of the seals. He shall be responsible for the records and be in charge of the publications of the Court of First Instance.

Article 27

Subject to Articles 5 and 33, the Registrar shall attend the sittings of the Court of First Instance and of the Chambers.

Section 2 – Other Departments

Article 28

The officials and other servants whose task is to assist directly the President, the Judges and the Registrar shall be appointed in accordance with the Staff Regulations. They shall be responsible to the Registrar, under the authority of the President of the Court of First Instance.

Article 29

The officials and other servants referred to in Article 28 shall take the oath provided for in Article 20 (2) of the Rules of Procedure of the Court of Justice before the President of the Court of First Instance in the presence of the Registrar.

Article 30

The Registrar shall be responsible, under the authority of the President of the Court of First Instance, for the administration of the Court of First Instance, its financial management and its accounts; he shall be assisted in this by the departments of the Court of Justice.

Chapter 4

The working of the Court of First Instance

Article 31

1) The dates and times of the sittings of the Court of First Instance shall be fixed by the President.
2) The Court of First Instance may choose to hold one or more sittings in a place other than that in which the Court of First Instance has its seat.

Article 32

1) Where, by reason of a Judge being absent or prevented from attending, there is an even number of Judges, the most junior Judge within the meaning of Article 6 shall abstain from taking part in the deliberations unless he is the Judge-Rapporteur. In this case, the Judge immediately senior to him shall abstain from taking part in the deliberations.

2) If, after the Court of First Instance has been convened in plenary session, it is found that the quorum of seven Judges has not been attained, the President of the Court of First Instance shall adjourn the sitting until there is a quorum.

3) If in any Chamber the quorum of three Judges has not been attained, the President of that Chamber shall so inform the President of the Court of First Instance who shall designate another Judge to complete the Chamber.

4) If in any Chamber of three or five Judges the number of Judges assigned to that Chamber is higher than three or five respectively, the President of the Chamber shall decide which of the Judges will be called upon to take part in the judgment of the case.

Article 33

1) The Court of First Instance shall deliberate in closed session.

2) Only those Judges who were present at the oral proceedings may take part in the deliberations.

3) Every Judge taking part in the deliberations shall state his opinion and the reasons for it.

4) Any Judge may require that any question be formulated in the language of his choice and communicated in writing to the other Judges before being put to the vote.

5) The conclusions reached by the majority of the Judges after final discussions shall determine the decision of the Court of First Instance. Votes shall be cast in reverse order to the order of precedence laid down in Article 6.

6) Differences in view of the substance, wording or order of questions, or on the interpretation of a vote shall be settled by decision of the Court of First Instance.

7) Where the deliberations of the Court of First Instance concern questions of its own administration, the Registrar shall be present, unless the Court of First Instance decides to the contrary.

8) Where the Court of First Instance sits without the Registrar being present it shall, if necessary, instruct the most junior Judge within the meaning of Article 6 to draw up minutes. The minutes shall be signed by this Judge and by the President.

Article 34

1) Subject to any special decision of the Court of First Instance, its vacations shall be as follows:
   – from 18 December to 10 January,
   – from the Sunday before Easter to the second Sunday after Easter,
   – from 15 July to 15 September.

During the vacations, the functions of President shall be exercised at the place where the Court of First Instance has its seat either by the President himself, keeping in touch with the Registrar, or by a President of Chamber or other Judge invited by the President to take his place.

2) In a case of urgency, the President may convene the Judges during the vacations.

3) The Court of First Instance shall observe the official holidays of the place where it has its seat.

4) The Court of First Instance may, in proper circumstances, grant leave of absence to any Judge.

Chapter 5

Languages

Article 35

1) The language of a case shall be Danish, Dutch, English, French, German, Greek, Irish, Italian, Portuguese or Spanish.

2) The language of the case shall be chosen by the applicant, except that:

   (a) at the joint request of the parties of the Court of First Instance may authorise another of the languages mentioned in paragraph (1) of this Article to be used as the language of the case for all or part of the proceedings;

   (b) at the request of one of the parties, and after the opposite party and the Advocate-General have been heard, the Court of First Instance may, by way of derogation from subparagraph (a), authorise another of the languages mentioned in paragraph (1) of this Article to be used as the language of the case for all or part of the proceedings; such a request may not be submitted by an institution.

3) The language of the case shall be used in the written and oral pleadings of the parties and in supporting documents, and also in the minutes and decisions of the Court of First Instance.

   Any supporting documents expressed in another language must be accompanied by a translation into the language of the case.

   In the case of lengthy documents, translations may be confined to extracts. However, the Court of First Instance may, of its own motion or at the request of a party, at any time call for a complete or fuller translation.

   Notwithstanding the foregoing provisions, a Member State shall be entitled to use its official language when intervening in a case before the Court of First Instance. This provision shall apply both to written statements and to oral addresses. The Registrar shall cause any such statement or address to be translated into the language of the case.

4) Where a witness or expert states that he is unable adequately to express himseslf in one of the languages referred to in paragraph (1) of this article, the Court of First Instance may authorise him to give his evidence in another language. The Registrar shall arrange for translation into the language of the case.

5) The President in conducting oral proceedings, the Judge-Rapporteur both in his preliminary report and in his report for the hearing, Judges and the Advocate-General in putting questions and the Advocate-General in delivering his opinion may use one of the languages referred to in paragraph (1) of this article other than the language of the case. The Registrar shall arrange for translation into the language of the case.

Article 36

1) The Registrar shall, at the request of any Judge, of the Advocate-General or of a party, arrange for anything said or written in the course of the proceedings before the Court of First Instance to be translated into the languages he chooses from those referred to in Article 35 (1).

2) Publications of the Court of First Instance shall be issued in the language referred to in Article 1 of Council Regulation No 1.

Article 37

The texts of documents drawn up in the language of the case or in any other language authorised by the Court of First Instance pursuant to Article 35 shall be authentic.

Chapter 6

Rights and obligations of agents, advisers and lawyers

Article 38

1) Agents representing a State or an institution, as well as advisers and lawyers, appearing before the Court of First Instance or before any judicial authority to which it has addressed letters rogatory, shall enjoy immunity in respect of words spoken or written by them concerning the case or the parties.

2) Agents, advisers and lawyers shall enjoy the following further privileges and facilities:

(a) papers and documents relating to the proceedings shall be exempt from both search and seizure; in the event of a dispute the customs officials or police may seal those papers and documents; they shall then be immediately forwarded to the Court of First Instance for inspection in the presence of the Registrar and of the person concerned;

(b) agents, advisers and lawyers shall be entitled to such allocation of foreign currency as may be necessary for the performance of their duties;

(c) agents, advisers and lawyers shall be entitled to travel in the course of duty without hindrance.

Article 39

In order to quality for the privileges, immunities and facilities specified in Article 38, persons entitled to them shall furnish proof of their status as follows:

(a) agents shall produce an official document issued by the State or institution which they represent; a copy of this document shall be forwarded without delay to the Registrar by the State or institution concerned;

(b) advisers and lawyers shall produce a certificate signed by the Registrar. The validity of this certificate shall be limited to a specified period, which may be extended or curtailed according to the length of the proceedings.

Article 40

The privileges, immunities and facilities specified in Article 38 are granted exclusively in the interests of the proper conduct of proceedings.

The Court of First Instance may waive the immunity where it considers that the proper conduct of proceedings will not be hindered thereby.

Article 41

1) Any adviser or lawyer whose conduct towards the Court of First Instance, the President, a Judge or the Registrar is incompatible with the dignity of the Court of First Instance, or who uses his rights for purposes other than those for which they were granted, may at any time be excluded from the proceedings by an order of the Court of First Instance; the person concerned shall be given an opportunity to defend himself.

The order shall have immediate effect.

2) Where an adviser or lawyer is excluded from the proceedings, the proceedings shall be suspended for a period fixed by the President in order to allow the party concerned to appoint another adviser or lawyer.

3) Decisions taken under this article may be rescinded.

Article 42

The provisions of this Chapter shall apply to university teachers who have a right of audience before the Court of First Instance in accordance with Article

20 of the ECSC Statute and Article 17 of the EEC and Euratom Statutes.

Title 2 **Procedure**

Chapter 1

Written procedure

Article 43

1) The original of every pleading must be signed by the party's agent or lawyer.

The original, accompanied by all annexes referred to therein, shall be lodged together with five copies for the Court of First Instance and a copy for every other party to the proceedings. Copies shall be certified by the party lodging them.

2) Institutions shall in addition produce, within time-limits laid down by the Court of First Instance, translations of all pleadings into the other languages provided for by Article 1 of Council Regulation No 1. The second paragraph of paragraph (1) of this article shall apply.

3) All pleadings bear a date. In the reckoning of time-limits for taking steps in proceeding only the date of lodgment at the Registry shall be taken into account.

4) To every pleading there shall be annexed a file containing the documents relied on in support of it, together with a schedule listing them.

5) Where in view of the length of a document only extracts from it are annexed to the pleading, the whole document or a full copy of it shall be lodged at the Registry.

Article 44

1) An application of the kind referred to in Article 22 of the ECSC Statute and Article 19 of the EEC and Euratom Statutes shall state:
   (a) the name and address of the applicant;
   (b) the designation of the party against whom the application is made;
   (c) the subject-matter of the proceedings and a summary of the pleas in law on which the application is based;
   (d) the form of order sought by the applicant;
   (e) where appropriate, the nature of any evidence offered in support.

2) For the purpose of the proceedings, the application shall state an address for service in the place where the Court of First Instance has its seat and the

name of the person who is authorised and has expressed willingness to accept service.

If the application does not comply with these requirements, all service on the party concerned for the purposes of the proceedings shall be effected, for so long as the defect has not been cured, by registered letter addressed to the agent or lawyer of that party. By way of derogation from Article 100, service shall then be deemed to have been duly effected by the lodging of the registered letter at the post office of the place where the Court of First Instance has its seat.

3) The lawyer acting for a party must lodge at the Registry a certificate that he is entitled to practise before a court of a Member State.

4) The application shall be accompanied, where appropriate, by the documents specified in the second paragraph of Article 22 of the ECSC Statute and in the second paragraph of Article 19 of the EEC and Euratom Statutes.

5) An application made by a legal person governed by private law shall be accompanied by:

   (a) the instrument or instruments constituting and regulating that legal person or a recent extract from the register of companies, firms or associations or any other proof of its existence in law;

   (b) proof that the authority granted to the applicant's lawyer has been properly conferred on him by someone authorised for the purpose.

6) If an application does not comply with the requirements set out in paragraphs (3) to (5) of this article, the Registrar shall prescribe a reasonable period within which the applicant is to comply with them whether by putting the application itself in order or by producing any of the abovementioned documents. If the applicant fails to put the application in order or to produce the required documents within the time prescribed, the Court of First Instance shall decide whether the non-compliance with these conditions renders the application formally inadmissible.

Article 45

The application shall be served on the defendant. In a case where Article 44 (6) applies, service shall be effected as soon as the application has been put in order or the Court of First Instance has declared it admissible notwithstanding the failure to observe the formal requirements set out in that Article.

Article 46

Within one month after service on him of the application, the defendant shall lodge a defence, stating:

(a) The name and address of the defendant;

(b) the arguments of fact and law relied on;

(c) the form of order sought by the defendant;

(d) the nature of any evidence offered by him.

The provisions of Article 44 (2) to (5) shall apply to the defence.

2) In proceedings between the Communities and their servants the defence shall be accompanied by the complaint within the meaning of Article 90 (2) of the Staff Regulation of Officials and by the decision rejecting the complaint together with the dates on which the complaint was submitted and the decision notified.

3) The time-limit laid down in paragraph (1) of this article may be extended by the President on a reasoned application by the defendant.

Article 47

1) The application initiating the proceedings and the defence may be supplemented by a reply from the applicant and by a rejoinder from the defendant.

2) The President shall fix the time-limits within which these pleadings are to be lodged.

Article 48

1) In reply or rejoinder a party may offer further evidence. The party must, however, give reasons for the delay in offering it.

2) No new plea in law may be introduced in the course of proceedings unless it is based on matters of law or of fact which come to light in the course of the procedure.

    If in the course of the procedure one of the parties puts forward a new plea in law which is so based, the President may, even after the expiry of the normal procedural time-limits, acting on a report of the Judge-Rapporteur and after hearing the Advocate-General, allow the other party time to answer on that plea.

    Consideration of the admissibility of the plea shall be reserved for the final judgment.

Article 49

At any stage of the proceedings the Court of First Instance may, after hearing the Advocate-General, prescribe any measure of organization of procedure or any measure of inquiry referred to in Articles 64 and 65 or order that a previous inquiry be repeated or expanded.

Article 50

The President may, at any time, after hearing the parties and the Advocate-

General, order that two or more cases concerning the same subject-matter shall, on account of the connection between them, be joined for the purposes of the written or oral procedure or of the final judgment. The cases may subsequently be disjoined.

Article 51

In the cases specified in Article 14, and at any stage in the proceedings, the Chamber hearing the case may, either on its own initiative or at the request of one of the parties, propose to the Court of First Instance sitting in plenary session that the case be referred to the Court of First Instance sitting in plenary session or to a Chamber composed of a different number of Judges. The Court of First Instance sitting in plenary session shall, after hearing the parties and the Advocate-General, decide whether or not to refer a case.

Article 52

1) Without prejudice to the application of Article 49, the President shall, after the rejoinder has been lodged, fix a date on which the Judge-Rapporteur is to present his preliminary report to the Court of First Instance. The report shall contain recommendations as to whether measures of organization of procedure or measures of inquiry should be undertaken and whether the case should be referred to the Court of First Instance sitting in plenary session or to a Chamber composed of a different number of Judges.

2) The Court of First Instance shall decide, after hearing the Advocate-General, what action to take upon the recommendations of the Judge-Rapporteur.

The same procedure shall apply:

(a) where no reply or no rejoinder has been lodged within the time-limit fixed in accordance with Article 47 (2);

(b) where the party concerned waives his right to lodge a reply or rejoinder.

Article 53

Where the Court of First Instance decides to open the oral procedure without undertaking measures of organization of procedure or ordering a preparatory inquiry, the President of the Court of First Instance shall fix the opening date.

Article 54

Without prejudice to any measures of organization of procedure or measures of inquiry which may be arranged at the stage of the oral procedure, where, during the written procedure, measures of organization or procedure or measures of inquiry have been instituted and completed, the President shall fix the date for the opening of the oral procedure.

Chapter 2

Oral procedure

Article 55

1) Subject to the priority of decisions provided for in Article 106, the Court of First Instance shall deal with the cases before it in the order in which the preparatory inquiries in them have been completed. Where the preparatory inquiries in several cases are completed simultaneously, the order in which they are to be dealt with shall be determined by the dates of entry in the register of the application is initiating them respectively.

2) The President may in special circumstances order that a case be given priority over others.

The President may in special circumstances, after hearing the parties and the Advocate-General, either on his own initiative or at the request of one of the parties, defer a case to be dealt with at a later date. On a joint application by the parties the President may order that a case be deferred.

Article 56

The proceedings shall be opened and directed by the President, who shall be responsible for the proper conduct of the hearing.

Article 57

The oral proceedings in cases heard *in camera* shall not be published.

Article 58

The President may in the course of the hearing put questions to the agents, advisers or lawyers of the parties.

The other Judges and the Advocate-General may do likewise.

Article 59

A party may address the Court of First Instance only through his agent, adviser or lawyer.

Article 60

Where an Advocate-General has not been designated in a case, the President shall declare the oral procedure closed at the end of the hearing.

Article 61

1) Where the Advocate-General delivers his opinion in writing, he shall lodge it at the Registry, which shall communicate it to the parties.
2) After the delivery, orally or in writing, of the opinion of the Advocate-General the President shall declare the oral procedure closed.

Article 62

The Court of First Instance may, after hearing the Advocate-General, order the re-opening of the oral procedure.

Article 63

1) The Registrar shall draw up minutes of every hearing. The minutes shall be signed by the President and by the Registrar and shall constitute an official record.
2) The parties may inspect the minutes at the Registry and obtain copies at their own expense.

Chapter 3

Measures of organization of procedure and measures of inquiry

Section 1 – Measures of organization of procedure

Article 64

1) The purpose of measures of organization of procedure shall be to ensure that cases are prepared for hearing, procedures carried out and disputes resolved under the best possible conditions. They shall be prescribed by the Court of First Instance, after hearing the Advocate-General.
2) Measures of organization of procedure shall, in particular, have as their purpose:
    (a) to ensure efficient conduct of the written and oral procedure and to facilitate the taking of evidence;
    (b) to determine the points on which the parties must present further argument or which call for measures of inquiry;
    (c) to clarify the forms of order sought by the parties, their pleas in law and arguments and the points at issue between them;
    (d) to facilitate the amicable settlement of proceedings.
    3) Measures of organization of procedure may, in particular, consist of:
    (a) putting questions to the parties;

(b) inviting the parties to make written or oral submissions on certain aspects of the proceedings;

(c) asking the parties or third parties for information or particulars;

(d) asking for documents or any papers relating to the case to be produced;

(e) summoning the parties' agents or the parties in person to meetings.

4) Each party may, at any stage of the procedure, propose the adoption or modification of measures of organization of procedure. In that case, the other parties shall be heard before those measures are prescribed.

Where the procedural circumstances so require, the Registrar shall inform the parties of the measures envisaged by the Court of First Instance and shall give them an opportunity to submit comments orally or in writing.

5) If the Court of First Instance sitting in plenary session decides to prescribe measures of organizaton of procedure and does not undertake such measures itself it shall entrust the task of so doing to the Chamber to which the case was originally assigned or to the Judge-Rapporteur.

If a Chamber prescribes measures of organization of procedure and does not undertake such measures itself, it shall entrust the task to the Judge-Rapporteur.

The Advocate-General shall take the part in measures of organization of procedure.

Section 2 – Measures of inquiry

Article 65

Without prejudice to Articles 24 and 25 of the ECSC Statues, Articles 21 and 22 of the EEC Statute or Articles 22 and 23 of the Euratom Statute, the following measures of inquiry may be adopted:

(a) the personal appearance of the parties;

(b) a request for information and production of documents;

(c) oral testimony;

(d) the commissioning of an expert's report;

(e) an inspection of the place or thing in question.

Article 66

1) The Court of First Instance, after hearing the Advocate-General, shall prescribe the measures of inquiry that it considers appropriate by means of an order setting out the facts to be proved. Before the Court of First Insance decides on the measures of inquiry referred to in Article 65 (c), (d) and (e) the parties shall be heard.

The order shall be served on the parties.

2) Evidence may be submitted in rebuttal and previous evidence may be amplified.

Article 67

1) Where the Court of First Instance sitting in plenary session orders a preparatory inquiry and does not undertake such an inquiry itself, it shall entrust the task of so doing to the Chamber to which the case was originally assigned or to the Judge-Rapporteur.

   Where a Chamber orders a preparatory inquiry and does not undertake such an inquiry itself, it shall entrust the task of so doing to the Judge-Rapporteur.

   The Advocate-General shall take part in the measures of inquiry.

2) The parties may be present at the measures of inquiry.

Section 3 – The summoning and examination of witnesses and experts

Article 68

1) The Court of First Instance may, either of its own motion or on application by a party, and after hearing the Advocate-General and the parties, order that certain facts be proved by witnesses. The order shall set out the facts to be established.

   The Court of First Instance may summon a witness of its own motion or on application by a party or at the instance of the Advocate-General.

   An applicaton by a party for the examination of a witness shall state precisely about what facts and for what reasons the witness should be examined.

2) The witness shall be summoned by an order containing the following information:

   (a) the surname, forenames, description and address of the witness;

   (b) an indication of the facts about which the witness is to be examined;

   (c) where appropriate, particulars of the arrangements made by the Court of First Instance for reimbursement of expenses incurred by the witness, and of the penalties which may be imposed on defaulting witnesses.

   The order shall be served on the parties and the witnesses.

3) The Court of First Instance may make the summoning of a witness for whose examination a party has applied conditional upon the deposit with the cashier of the Court of First Instance of a sum sufficient to cover the taxed costs thereof; the Court of First Instance shall fix the amount of the payment.

The cashier of the Court of First Instance shall advance the funds necessary in connexion with the examination of any witness summoned by the Court of First Instance of is own motion.

4) After the identity of the witness has been established, the President shall inform him that he will be required to vouch the truth of his evidence in the manner laid down in paragraph (5) of this Article and in Article 71.

The witness shall give his evidence to the Court of First Instance, the parties having been given notice to attend. After the witness has given his main evidence the President may, at the request of a party or of his own motion, put questions to him.

The other Judges and the Advocate-General may do likewise.

Subject to the control of the President, questions may be put to witnesses by the representatives of the parties.

5) Subject to the provisions of Article 71, the witness shall, after giving his evidence, take the following oath:

"I swear that I have spoken the truth, the whole truth and nothing but the truth."

The Court of First Instance may, after hearing the parties, exempt a witness from taking the oath.

6) The Registrar shall draw up minutes in which the evidence of each witness is reproduced.

The minutes shall be signed by the President or by the Judge-Rapporteur responsible for conducting the examination of the witness, and by the Registrar. Before the minutes are thus signed, witnesses must be given an opportunity to check the content of the minutes and to sign them.

The minutes shall constitute an official record.

Article 69

1) Witnesses who have been duly summoned shall obey the summons and attend for examination.

2) If a witness who has been duly summoned fails to appear before the Court of First Instance, the latter may impose upon him a pecuniary penalty not exceeding 5 000 ECU and may order that a further summons be served on the witness at his own expense.

The same penalty may be imposed upon a witness who, without good reason, refuses to give evidence or to take the oath or where appropriate to make a solemn affirmation equivalent thereto.

3) If the witness proffers a valid excuse to the Court of First Instance, the pecuniary penalty imposed on him may be cancelled. The pecuniary penalty imposed may be reduced at the request of the witness where he establishes that it is disproportionate to his income.

4) Penalties imposed and other measures ordered under this Article shall be enforced in accordance with Articles 44 and 92 of the ECSC Treaty, Articles 187 and 192 of the EEC Treaty and Articles 159 and 164 of the Euratom Treaty.

Article 70

1) The Court of First Instance may order that an expert's report be obtained. The order appointing the expert shall define his task and set a time-limit within which he is to make his report.
2) The expert shall receive a copy of the order, together with all the documents necessary for carrying out his task. He shall be under the supervision of the Judge-Rapporteur, who may be present during his investigation and who shall be kept informed of his progress in carrying out his task.
   The Court of First Instance may request the parties or one of them to lodge security for the costs of the expert's report.
3) At the request of the expert, the Court of First Instance may order the examination of witnesses. Their examination shall be carried out in accordance with Article 68.
4) The expert may give his opinion only on points which have been expressly referred to him.
5) After the expert has made his report, the Court of First Instance may order that he be examined, the parties having been given notice to attend.
   Subject to the control of the President, questions may be put to the expert by the representatives of the parties.
6) Subject to the provisions of Article 71, the expert shall, after making his report, take the following oath before the Court of First Instance: "I swear that I have conscientiously and impartially carried out my task."
   The Court of First Instance may, after hearing the parties, exempt the expert from taking the oath.

Article 71

1) The President shall instruct any person who is required to take an oath before the Court of First Instance, as witness or expert, to tell the truth or to carry out his task conscientiously and impartially, as the case may be, and shall warn him of the criminal liability provided for in his national law in the event of any breach of this duty.
2) Witnesses and experts shall take the oath either in accordance with the first subparagraph of Article 68 (5) and the first subparagraph of Article 70 (6) or in the manner laid down by their national law.

3) Where the national law provides the opportunity to make, in judicial proceedings, a solemn affirmation equivalent to an oath as well as orinstead of taking an oath, the witnesses and experts may make such an affirmation under the conditions and in the form prescribed in their national law.

Where their national law provides neither for taking an oath nor for making a solemn affirmation, the procedure described in the first paragraph of this article shall be followed.

Article 72

1) The Court of First Instance may, after hearing the Advocate-General, decide to report to the competent authority referred to in Annex III to the Rules supplementing the Rules of Procedure of the Court of Justice of the Member State whose courts have penal jurisdiction in any case of perjury on the part of a witness or expert before the Court of First Instance, account being taken of the provisions of Article 71.

2) The Registrar shall be responsible for communicating the decision of the Court of First Instance. The decision shall set out the facts and circumstances on which the report is based.

Article 73

1) If one of the parties objects to a witness or to an expert on the ground that he is not a competent or proper person to act as witness or expert or for any other reason, or if a witness or expert refuses to give evidence, to take the oath or to make a solemn affirmation equivalent thereto, the matter shall be resolved by the Court of First Instance.

2) An objection to a witness or to an expert shall be raised within two weeks after service of the order summoning the witness or appointing the expert; the statement of objection must set out the grounds of objection and indicate the nature of any evidence offered.

Article 74

1) Witnesses and experts shall be entitled to reimbursement of their travel and subsistence expenses. The cashier of the Court of First Instance may make a payment to them towards these expenses in advance.

2) Witnesses shall be entitled to compensation for loss of earnings, and experts to fees for their services. The cashier of the Court of First Instance shall pay

witnesses and experts their compensation or fees after they have carried out their respective duties or tasks.

Article 75

1) The Court of First Instance may, on application by a party or of its own motion, issue letters rogatory for the examination of witnesses or experts.
2) Letters rogatory shall be issued in the form of an order which shall contain the name, forenames, description and address of the witness or expert, set out the facts on which the witness or expert is to be examined, name the parties, their agents, lawyers or advisers, indicate their addresses for service and briefly describe the subject-matter of the proceedings.

   Notice of the order shall be served on the parties by the Registrar.
3) The Registrar shall send the order to the competent authority named in Annex I to the Rules supplementing the Rules of Procedure of the Court of Justice of the Member State in whose territory the witness or expert is to be examined. Where necessary, the order shall be accompanied by a translation into the official language or languages of the Member State to which it is addressed.

   The authority named pursuant to the first paragraph shall pass on the order to the judicial authority which is competent according to its national law.

   The competent judicial authority shall give effect to the letters rogatory in accordance with its national law. After implementation the competent judicial authority shall transmit to the authority named pursuant to the first paragraph the order embodying the letters rogatory, any documents arising from the implementation and a detailed statement of costs. These documents shall be sent to the Registrar.

   The Registrar shall be responsible for the translation of the documents into the language of the case.
4) The Court of First Instance shall defray the expenses occasioned by the letters rogatory without prejudice to the right to charge them, where appropriate, to the parties.

Article 76

1) The Registrar shall draw up minutes of every hearing. The minutes shall be signed by the President and by the Registrar and shall constitute an official record.
2) The parties may inspect the minutes and any expert's report at the Registry and obtain copies at their own expense.

Chapter 4

Stay of proceedings and declining of jurisdiction by the Court of First Instance

Article 77

Without prejudice to Article 123 (4), Article 128 and Article 129 (4), proceedings may be stayed:

(a) in the circumstances specified in the third paragraph of Article 47 of the ECSC Statute, the third paragraph of Article 47 of the EEC Statute and the third paragraph of Article 48 of the Euratom Statute;

(b) where an appeal is brought before the Court of Justice against a decision of the Court of First Instance disposing of the substantive issues in part only, disposing of a procedural issue concerning a plea of lack of competence or inadmissibility or dismissing an application to intervene;

(c) at the joint request of the parties.

Article 78

The decision to stay the proceedings shall be made by order of the Court of First Instance, after hearing the parties and the Advocate-General. The Court of First Instance may, following the same procedure, order that the proceedings be resumed. The orders referred to in this article shall be served on the parties.

Article 79

1) The stay of proceedings shall take effect on the date indicated in the order of stay or, in the absence of such an indication, on the date of that order. While proceedings are stayed time shall, except for the purposes of the time-limit prescribed in Article 115 (1) for an application to intervene, cease to run for the purposes of prescribed time-limits for all parties.

2) Where the order or stay does not fix the length of the stay, it shall end on the date indicated in the order of resumption or, in the absence of such indication, on the date of the order of resumption. From the date of resumption time shall begin to run afresh for the purposes of the time-limits.

Article 80

Decisions declining jurisdiction in the circumstances specified in the third paragraph of Article 47 of the ECSC Statute, the third paragraph of Article 47 of the EEC Statute and the third paragraph of Article 48 of the Euratom

Statute shall be made by the Court of First Instance by way of an order which shall be served on the parties.

Chapter 5

Judgments

Article 81
The judgment shall contain:
– a statement that it is the judgment of the Court of First Instance,
– the date of its delivery,
– the names of the President and of the Judges taking part in it,
– the name of the Advocate-General, if designated,
– the name of the Registrar,
– the description of the parties,
– the names of the agents, advisers and lawyers of the parties,
– a statement of the forms of order sought by the parties,
– a statement, where appropriate, that the Advocate-General delivered his opinion,
– a summary of the facts,
– the grounds for the decision,
– the operative part of the judgment, including the decision as to costs.

Article 82
1) The judgment shall be delivered in open court; the parties shall be given notice to attend to hear it.
2) The original of the judgment, signed by the President, by the Judges who took part in the deliberations and by the Registrar, shall be sealed and deposited at the Registry; the parties shall be served with certified copies of the judgment.
3) The Registrar shall record on the original of the judgment the date on which it was delivered.

Article 83
Subject to the provisions of the second paragraph of Article 53 of the ECSC Statute, the second paragraph of Article 53 of the EEC Statute and the second paragraph of Article 54 of the Euratom Statute, the judgment shall be binding from the date of its delivery.

Article 84
1) Without prejudice to the provisions, relating to the interpretation of judg-

ments, the Court of First Instance may, of its own motion or on application by a party made within two weeks after the delivery of a judgment, rectify clerical mistakes, errors in calculation and obvious slips in it.

2) The parties, whom the Registrar shall duly notify, may lodge written observations within a period prescribed by the President.

3) The Court of First Instance shall take its decision in closed session.

4) The original of the rectification order shall be annexed to the original of the rectified judgment. A note of this order shall be made in the margin of the original of the rectified judgment.

Article 85

If the Court of First Instance should omit to give a decision on costs, any party may within a month after service of the judgment apply to the Court of First Instance to supplement its judgment.

The application shall be served on the opposite party and the President shall prescribe a period within which that party may lodge written observations. After these observations have been lodged, the Court of First Instance shall decide both on the admissibility and on the substance of the application.

Article 86

The Registrar shall arrange for the publication of cases before the Court of First Instance.

Chapter 6

Costs

Article 87

1) A decision as to costs shall be given in the final judgment or in the order which closes the proceedings.

2) The unsuccessful party shall be ordered to pay the costs if they have been applied for in the successful party's pleadings.

   Where there are several unsuccessful parties the Court of First Instance shall decide how the costs are to be shared.

3) Where each party succeeds on some and fails on other heads, or where the circumstances are exceptional, the Court of First Instance may order that the costs be shared or that each party bear its own costs.

   The Court of First Instance may order a party, even if successful, to pay costs which it considers that party to have unreasonably or vexatiously caused the opposite party to incur.

4) The Member States and institutions which intervened in the proceedings shall bear their own costs

The Court of First Instance may order an intervener other than those mentioned in the preceding subparagraph to bear his own costs.

5) A party who discontinues or withdraws from proceedings shall be ordered to pay the costs if they have been applied for in the other party's pleadings. However, upon application by the party who discontinues or withdraws from proceedings, the costs shall be borne by the other party if this appears justified by the conduct of that party.

Where the parties have come to an agreement on costs, the decision as to costs shall be in accordance with that agreement.

If costs are not claimed in the written pleadings, the parties shall bear their own costs.

6) Where a case does not proceed to judgment, the costs shall be in the discretion of the Court of First Instance.

Article 88

Without prejudice to the second subparagraph of Article 87 (3), in proceedings between the Communities and their servants the institutions shall bear their own costs.

Article 89

Costs necessarily incurred by a party in enforcing a judgment or order of the Court of First Instance shall be refunded by the opposite party on the scale in force in the State where the enforcement takes place.

Article 90

Proceedings before the Court of First Instance shall be free of charge, except that:

(a) where a party has caused the Court of First Instance to incur avoidable costs, the Court of First Instance may order that party to refund them;

(b) where copying or translation work is carried out at the request of a party, the cost shall, in so far as the Registrar considers it excessive, be paid for by that party on the scale of charges referred to in Article 24 (5).

Article 91

Without prejudice to the preceding article, the following shall be regarded as recoverable costs:

(a) sums payable to witnesses and experts under Article 74;

(b) expenses necessarily incurred by the parties for the purpose of the proceedings, in particular the travel and subsistence expenses and the remuneration of agents, advisers or lawyers.

Article 92

1) If there is a dispute concerning the costs to be recovered, the Court of First Instance hearing the case shall, on application by the party concerned and after hearing the opposite party, make an order, from which no appeal shall lie.

2) The parties may, for the purposes of enforcement, apply for an authenticated copy of the order.

Article 93

1) Sums due from cashier of the Court of First Instance shall be paid in the currency of the country where the Court of First Instance has its seat.
At the request of the person entitled to any sum, it shall be paid in the currency of the country where the expenses to be refunded were incurred or where the steps in respect of which payment is due were taken.

2) Other debtors shall make payment in the currency of their country of origin.

3) Conversions of currency shall be made at the official rates of exchange ruling on the day of payment in the country where the Court of First Instance has its seat.

Chapter 7

Legal aid

Article 94

1) A party who is wholly or in part unable to meet the costs of the proceedings may at any time apply for legal aid.
The application shall be accompanied by evidence of the applicant's need of assistance, and in particular by a document from the competent authority certifying his lack of means.

2) If the application is made prior to proceedings which the applicant wishes to commence, it shall briefly state the subject of such proceedings.
The application need not be made through a lawyer.
The President of the Court of First Instance shall designate a Judge to act as Rapporteur. The Chamber to which the latter belongs shall, after considering the written observations of the opposite party, decide whether legal aid should be granted in full or in part, or whether it should be refused. The Chamber shall consider whether there is manifestly no cause of action.
The Chamber shall make an order without giving reasons, and no appeal shall lie therefrom.

Article 95

1) The Court of First Instance, by any order by which it decides that a person is entitled to receive legal aid, shall order that a lawyer be appointed to act for him.
2) If the person does not indicate his choice of lawyer, or if the Court of First Instance considers that his choice is unacceptable, the Registrar shall send a copy of the order and of the application for legal aid to the authority named in Annex II to the Rules supplementing the Rules of Procedure of the Court of Justice, being the competent authority of the State concerned.
3) The Court of First Instance, in the light of the suggestions made by that authority, shall of its own motion appoint a lawyer to act for the person concerned.

Article 96

The Court of First Instance may at any time, either of its own motion or on application, withdraw legal aid if the circumstances which led to its being granted alter during the proceedings.

Article 97

1) Where legal aid is granted, the cashier of the Court of First Instance shall advance the funds necessary to meet the expenses.
2) The Court of First Instance shall adjudicate on the lawyer's disbursements and fees; the President may, on application by the lawyer, order that he receive an advance.
3) In its decision as to costs the Court of First Instance may order the payment to the cashier of the Court of First Instance of the whole or any part of amounts advanced as legal aid.
   The Registrar shall take steps to obtain the recovery of these sums from the party ordered to pay them.

Chapter 8

Discontinuance

Article 98

If, before the Court of First Instance has given its decision, the parties reach a settlement of their dispute and intimate to the Court of First Instance the abandonment of their claims, the President shall order the case to be removed from the register and shall give a decision as to costs in accordance with Article

87 (5) having regard to any proposals made by the parties on the matter. This provision shall not apply to proceedings under Articles 33 and 35 of the ECSC Treaty, Articles 173 and 175 of the EEC Treaty or Articles 146 and 148 of the Euratom Treaty.

Article 99

If the applicant informs the Court of First Instance in writing that he wishes to discontinue the proceedings, the President shall order the case to be removed from the register and shall give a decision as to costs in accordance with Article 87 (5).

Chapter 9

Service

Article 100

Where these Rules require that a document be served on a person, the Registrar shall ensure that service is effected at that person's address for service either by the dispatch of a copy of the document by registered post with a form for acknowledgment of receipt or by personal delivery of the copy against a receipt.

The Registrar shall prepare and certify the copies of documents to be served, save where the parties themselves supply the copies in accordance with Article 43 (1).

Chapter 10

Time-limits

Article 101

1) Any period of time prescribed by the ECSC, EEC or Euratom Treaties, the Statutes of the Court of Justice or these Rules for the taking of any procedural step shall be reckoned as follows:

   (a) Where a period expressed in days, weeks, months or years is to be calculated from the moment at which an event occurs or an action takes place, the day during which that event occurs or that action takes place shall not be counted as falling within the period in question;

   (b) A period expressed in weeks, months or in years shall end with the expiry of whichever day in the last week, month or year is the same day of the week, or falls on the same date, as the day during which the event or action from which the period is to be calculated occurred or took place. If, in a period expressed in months or in years, the day on which it should expire does not occur in the last month, the period shall end with the expiry of the last day of that month;

(c) Where a period is expressed in months and days, it shall first be reckoned in whole months, then in days;

(d) Periods shall include official holidays, Sundays and Saturdays;

(e) Periods shall not be suspended during the judicial vacations.

2) If the period would otherwise end on a Saturday, Sunday or official holiday, it shall be extended until the end of the first following working day.

The list of official holidays drawn up by the Court of Justice and published in the *Official Journal of the European Communities* shall apply to the Court of First Instance.

Article 102

1) The period of time allowed for commencing proceedings against a measure adopted by an institution shall run from the day following the receipt by the person concerned of notification of the measure or, where the measure is published, from the 15th day after publication thereof in the *Official Journal of the European Communities*.

2) The extensions, on account of distance, of prescribed time-limits provided for in a decision of the Court of Justice and published in the *Official Journal of the European Communities* shall apply to the Court of First Instance.

Article 103

1) Any time-limit prescribed pursuant to these Rules may be extended by whoever prescribed it.

2) The President may delegate power of signature to the Registrar for the purpose of fixing time-limits which, pursuant to these Rules, it falls to the President to prescribe, or of extending such time-limits.

Title 3 Special forms of procedure

Chapter 1

Suspension of operation or enforcement and other interim measures

Article 104

1) An application to suspend the operation of any measure adopted by an

institution, made pursuant to the second paragraph of Article 39 of the ECSC Treaty, Article 185 of the EEC Treaty or Article 157 of the Euratom Treaty, shall be admissible only if the applicant is challenging that measure in proceedings before the Court of First Instance.

An application for the adoption of any other interim measure referred to in the third paragraph of Article 39 of the ECSC Treaty, Article 186 of the EEC Treaty or Article 158 of the Euratom Treaty shall be admissible only if it is made by a party to a case before the Court of First Instance and relates to that case.

2) An application of a kind of referred to in paragraph (1) of this Article shall state the subject-matter of the proceedings, the circumstances giving rise to urgency and the pleas of fact and law establishing a *prima facie* case for the interim measures applied for.

3) The application shall be made by a separate document and in accordance with the provision of Articles 43 and 44.

Article 105

1) The application shall be served on the opposite party, and the President of the Court of First Instance shall prescribe a short period within which that party may submit written or oral observations.

2) The President of the Court of First Instance may order a preparatory inquiry.

The President of the Court of First Instance may grant the application even before the observations of the opposite party have been submitted. This decision may be varied or cancelled even without any application being made by any party.

Article 106

The President of the Court of First Instance shall either decide on the application himself or refer it to the Chamber to which the case has been assigned in the main proceedings or to the Court of First Instance sitting in plenary session if the case has been assigned to it.

If the President of the Court of First Instance is absent or prevented from attending, he shall be replaced by the President of the most senior Judge, within the meaning of Article 6, of the bench of the Court of First Instance to which the case has been assigned.

Where the application is referred to a bench of the Court of First Instance, that bench shall postpone all other cases and shall give a decision. Article 105 shall apply.

Article 107

1) The decision on the application shall take the form of a reasoned order.

The order shall be served on the parties forthwith.

2) The enforcement of the order may be made conditional on the lodging by the applicant of security, of an amount and nature to be fixed in the light of the circumstances.

3) Unless the order fixes the date on which the interim measure is to lapse, the measure shall lapse when final judgment is delivered.

4) The order shall have only an interim effect, and shall be without prejudice to the decision on the substance of the case by the Court of First Instance.

Article 108

On application by a party, the order may at any time be varied or cancelled on account of a change in circumstances.

Article 109

Rejection of an application for an interim measure shall not bar the party who made it from making a further application on the basis of new facts.

Article 110

The provisions of this Chapter shall apply to applications to suspend the enforcement of a decision of the Court of First Instance or of any measure adopted by another institution, submitted pursuant to Articles 44 and 92 of the ECSC Treaty, Articles 187 and 192 of the EEC Treaty or Articles 159 and 164 of the Euratom Treaty.

The order granting the application shall fix, where appropriate, a date on which the interim measure is to lapse.

Chapter 2

Preliminary issues

Article 111

Where it is clear that the Court of First Instance has no jurisdiction to take cognizance of an action or where the action is manifestly inadmissible, the Court of First Instance may, by reasoned order, after hearing the Advocate-General and without taking further steps in the proceedings, give a decision on the action.

Article 112

The decision to refer an action to the Court of Justice, pursuant to the second paragraph of Article 47 of the ECSC Statute, the second paragraph of Article 47 of the EEC Statute and the second paragraph of Article 48 of the Euratom

Statute, shall, in the case of manifest lack of competence, be made by reasoned order and without taking any further steps in the proceedings.

Article 113

The Court of First Instance may at any time of its own motion consider whether there exists any absolute bar to proceeding with it, and shall give its decision in accordance with Article 114 (3) and (4).

Article 114

1) A party applying to the Court of First Instance for a decision on admissibility, on lack of competence or other preliminary plea not going to the substance of the case shall make the application by a separate document. The application must contain the pleas of fact and law relied on and the form of order sought by the applicant; any supporting documents must be annexed to it.

2) As soon as the application has been lodged, the President shall prescribe a period within which the opposite party may lodge a document containing a statement of the form of order sought by that party and its pleas in law.

3) Unless the Court of First Instance otherwise decides, the remainder of the proceedings shall be oral.

4) The Court of First Instance shall, after hearing the Advocate-General, decide on the application or reserve its decision for the final judgment. It shall refer the case to the Court of Justice if the case falls within the jurisdiction of that Court.

   If the Court of First Instance refuses the application or reserves its decision, the President shall prescribe new time-limits for further steps in the proceedings.

Chapter 3

Intervention

Article 115

1) An application to intervene must be made within three months of the publication of the notice referred to in Article 24 (6).

2) The application shall contain:
   (a) the description of the case;
   (b) the description of the parties;
   (c) the name and address of the intervener;
   (d) the intervener's address for service at the place where the Court of First Instance has its seat;

(e) the form of order sought, by one or more of the parties, in support of which the intervener is applying for leave to intervene;

(f) except in the case of applications to intervene made by Member States or institutions, a statement of the reasons establishing the intervener's interest in the result of the case.

Articles 43 and 44 shall apply.

3) The intervener shall be represented in accordance with the first and second paragraph of Article 20 of the ECSC Statute and with Article 17 of the EEC and Euratom Statutes.

Article 116

1) The application shall be served on the parties.

The President shall give the parties an opportunity to submit their written or oral observations before deciding on the application.

The President shall decide on the application by order or shall refer the decision to the Court of First Instance. The order must be reasoned if the application is dismissed.

2) If the President allows the intervention, the intervener shall receive a copy of every document served on the parties. The President may, however, on application by one of the parties, omit secret or confidential documents.

3) The intervener must accept the case as he find it at the time of his intervention.

4) The President shall prescribe a period within which the intervener may submit a statement in intervention.

The statement in intervention shall contain:

(a) a statment of the form of order sought by the intervener in support of or opposing, in whole or in part, the form of order sought by one of the parties;

(b) the pleas in law and arguments relied on by the intervener;

(c) where appropriate, the nature of any evidence offered.

5) After the statement in intervention has been lodged, the President shall, where necessary, prescribe a time-limit within which the parties may reply to that statement.

Chapter 4

Judgments of the Court of First Instance delivered after its decision has been set aside and the case referred back to it

Article 117

Where the court of Justice sets aside a judgment or an order of the Court of

First Instance and refers the case back to that Court, the latter shall be seised of the case by the judgment so referring it.

Article 118

1) Where the Court of Justice sets aside a judgment or an order of a Chamber, the President of the Court of First Instance may assign the case to another Chamber composed of the same number of Judges.

2) Where the Court of Justice sets aside a judgment delivered or an order made by the Court of First Instance sitting in plenary session, the case shall be assigned to that Court as so constituted.

3) In the cases provided for in paragraphs (1) and (2) of this article, Articles 13 (2), 14 and 51 shall apply.

Article 119

1) Where the written procedure before the Court of First Instance has been completed when the judgment referring the case back to it is delivered, the course of the procedure shall be as follows:

    (a) Within two months from the service upon him of the judgment of the Court of Justice the applicant may lodge a statement of written observations.

    (b) In the month following the communication to him of that statement, the defendant may lodge a statement of written observations. The time allowed to the defendant for lodging it may in no case be less than two months from the service upon him of the judgment of the Court of Justice.

    (c) In the month following the simultaneous communication to the intervener of the observations of the applicant and the defendant, the intervener may lodge a statement of written observations. The time allowed to the intervener for lodging it may in no case be less than two months from the service upon him of the judgment of the Court of Justice.

2) Where the written procedure before the Court of First Instance had not been completed when the judgment referring the case back to the Court of First Instance was delivered, it shall be resumed, at the stage which it had reached, by means of measures of organization of procedure adopted by the Court of First Instance.

3) The Court of First Instance may, if the circumstances so justify, allow supplementary statements of written observations to be lodged.

Article 120

The procedure shall be conducted in accordance with the provisions of Title II of these Rules.

Article 121

The Court of First Instance shall decide on the costs relating to the proceedings instituted before it and to the proceedings on the appeal before the Court of Justice.

Chapter 5

Judgments by default and applications to set them aside

Article 122

1) If a defendant on whom an application initiating proceedings has been duly served fails to lodge a defence to the application in the proper form within the time prescribed, the applicant may apply to the Court of First Instance for judgment by default.

   The application shall be served on the defendant. The President shall fix a date for the opening of the oral procedure.

2) Before giving judgment by default the Court of First Instance shall consider whether the application initiating proceedings is admissible, whether the appropriate formalities have been complied with, and whether the application appears well founded. It may order a preparatory inquiry.

3) A judgment by default shall be enforceable. The Court of First Instance may, however, grant a stay of execution until it has given its decision on any application under paragraph (4) of this Article to set aside the judgment, or it may make the execution subject to the provision of security of an amount and nature to be fixed in the light of the circumstances; this security shall be released if no such application is made or if the application fails.

4) Application may be made to set aside a judgment by default.

   The application to set aside the judgment must be made within one month from the date of service of the judgment and must be lodged in the form prescribed by Articles 43 and 44.

5) After the application has been served, the President shall prescribe a period within which the other party may submit his written observations.

   The proceedings shall be conducted in accordance with the provisions of Title II of these Rules.

6) The Court of First Instance shall decide by way of a judgment which may

not be set aside. The original of this judgment shall be annexed to the original of the judgment by default. A note of the judgment on the application to set aside shall be made in the margin of the original of the judgment by default.

Chapter 6

Exceptional review procedures

Section 1 – Third-party proceedings

Article 123

1) Articles 43 and 44 shall apply to an application initiating third-party proceedings. In addition such an application shall:
   (a) specify the judgment contested;
   (b) state how that judgment is prejudicial to the rights of the third party;
   (c) indicate the reasons for which the third party was unable to take part in the original case before the Court of First Instance.
   The application must be made against all the parties to the original case.
   Where the judgment has been published in the *Official Journal of the European Communities*, the application must be lodged within two months of the publication.
2) The Court of First Instance may, on application by the third party, order a stay of execution of the judgment. The provisions of Title III, Chapter 1, shall apply.
3) The contested judgment shall be varied on the points on which the submissions of the third party are upheld.
   The original of the judgment in the third-party proceedings shall be annexed to the original of the contested judgment. A note of the judgment in the third-party proceedings shall be made in the margin of the original of the contested judgment.
4) Where an appeal before the Court of Justice and an application initiating third-party proceedings before the Court of First Instance contest the same judgment of the Court of First Instance, the Court of First Instance may, after hearing the parties, stay the proceedings until the Court of Justice has delivered its judgment.

Article 124

The application initiating third-party proceedings shall be assigned to the Chamber which delivered the judgment which is the subject of the application; if the Court of First Instance sitting in plenary session delivered the judgment, the application shall be assigned to it.

Section 2 – Revision

Article 125

Without prejudice to the period of ten years prescribed in the third paragraph of Article 38 of the ECSC Statute, the third paragraph of Article 41 of the EEC Statute and the third paragraph of Article 42 of the Euratom Statute, an application for revision of a judgment shall be made within three months of the date on which the facts on which the application is based came to the applicant's knowledge.

Article 126

1) Articles 43 and 44 shall apply to an application for revision. In addition such an application shall:
   (a) specify the judgment contested;
   (b) indicate the points on which the application is based;
   (c) set out the facts on which the application is based;
   (d) indicate the nature of the evidence to show that there are facts justifying revison of the judgment, and that the time-limits laid down in Article 125 have been observed.
2) The application must be made against all partiess to the case in which the contested judgment was given.

Article 127

1) The application for revision shall be assigned to the Chamber which delivered the judgment which is the subject of the application; if the Court of First Instance sitting in plenary session delivered the judgment, the application shall be assigned to it.
2) Without prejudice to its decision on the substance, the Court of First Instance shall, after hearing the Advocate-General, having regard to the written observations of the parties, give its decision on the admissibility of the application
3) If the Court of First Instance finds the application admissible, it shall proceed to consider the substance of the application and shall give its decision in the form of a judgment in accordance with these Rules.
4) The original of the revising judgment shall be annexed to the original of the judgment revised. A note of the revising judgment shall be made in the margin of the original of the judgment revised.

Article 128
Where an appeal before the Court of Justice and an application for revision before the Court of First Instance concern the same judgment of the Court of First Instance, the Court of First Instance may, after hearing the parties, stay the proceedings until the Court of Justice has delivererd its judgment.

Section 3 – Interpretation of judgments

Article 129
1) An application for interpretation of a judgment shall be made in accordance with Articles 43 and 44. In addition it shall specify:
   (a) the judgment in question;
   (b) the passages of which interpretation is sought.
      The application must be made against all the parties to the case in which the judgment was given.
2) The application for interpretation shall be assigned to the Chamber which delivered the judgment which is the subject of the application; if the Court of First Instance sitting in plenary session delivered judgment, the application shall be assigned to it.
3) The Court of First Instance shall give its decision in the form of a judgment after having given the parties an opportunity to submit their observations and after hearing the Advocate-General.
   The original of the interpreting judgment shall be annexed to the original of the judgment interpreted. A note of the interpreting judgment shall be made in the margin of the original of the judgment interpreted.
4) Where an appeal before the Court of Justice and an application for interpretation before the Court of First Instance concern the same judgment of the Court of First Instance, the Court of First Instance may, after hearing the parties, stay the proceedings until the Court of Justice has delivered its judgment.

Miscellaneous provisions

Article 130
These Rules, which are authentic in the languages mentioned in Article 35 (1), shall be published in the *Official Journal of the European Communities*. They shall enter into force on the first day of the second month from the date of their publication.

*2 May 1991. OJ 1991 L 136.1.

Index